CAROLE WILEY
AN EVERYDAY HOUSEWIFE

**One Womans Response
to the War in Bosnia**

D0921096

Tom Keith

Published by
Miribride Publications
45 Liosbourne, Carrigaline, Co. Cork, Eire

Tel: 353-21-372670
353-58-41087

Printed by Litho Press Co., Midleton, Co. Cork.

Contents

To the brave people of Bosnia,
and the generous people of Ireland.

I do not boast of preaching the gospel, since it is a duty which has been laid on me; I should be punished if I did not preach it! If I had chosen this work myself, I might have been paid for it, but as I have not, it is a responsibility which has been put into my hands. Do you know what my reward is? It is this: in my preaching, to be able to offer the Good News free, and not insist on the rights which the gospel gives me.

Paul. 1 Cor. 9:16-18.

CAROLE WILEY

FOREWORD

This is the story of Carole Wiley who is, in her own words "an everyday housewife up to a point".

It is the simple story of one woman's response to the suffering of a people she knew well and is an extension of what she has been doing for the people of several mission countries.

It is not a story of the reported apparitions in Medjugorje. It is not the story of the war for independence in Bosnia/Hercegovina or the many atrocities which have been, and continue to be, committed by people of different religions and none.

The everyday duties of wife and mother, the care of her husband, home and children, the endless cycle of meals, washing and wash-up did not deter her from doing what she felt had to be done.

Without the events of the eighties in Medjugorje, the reported apparitions of the Blessed Virgin to six young residents of the Village, there would have been no reason for Áine Burke to travel there.

Without the war in Bosnia there would have been no heart-rending plea from Áine to Carole for much-needed medicines, food and clothes to care for a people brutalised beyond belief by a conflict that few of them understand fully.

Without that phone call there would not have been the super-human effort which has seen hundreds of thousands of pounds of desperately needed supplies flood into Carole's warehouse in Cork.

This is the story of that effort by one woman, supported by her family, a few close and loyal friends and the wider Irish public, which was to inspire people all over the country to work for the stricken families of Bosnia.

Many were people who had never been to Medjugorje and who probably never would, but who were spurred to action by horrific newsreel and reports that "a woman in Cork" was collecting for the people there.

This book does not purport to be an in-depth study of the war in Bosnia-Hercegovina, having been written at a considerable distance from where the events were taking place. This account of the war and some of the atrocities committed in the last two years is compiled from a variety of sources , including first-hand accounts given to Carole Wiley by residents of and visitors to that country, on her several visits there in the last year and a half; newsreel and video footage from Bosnia-Hercegovina and research in contemporary publications.

These are the views and opinions of Carole Wiley and the author, on the war in Bosnia-Hercegovina. If together they present a broadly accurate picture of conditions there over the last two years, then writing this book will have been worthwhile.

The purpose of the book is to continue to highlight the suffering of the people of all ethnic backrounds there; acknowledge the exceptional generosity of the Irish people towards their suffering sisters and brothers , and further promote the work of Carole Wiley and the other aid workers who are making a genuine and honest effort to help the victims of the war.

So the story of Medjugorje is the story of Bosnia, which is also the story of the friendship of two Irishwomen forged on the slopes of Apparition Hill, which was to bring some solace and a glimmer of hope to a simple people, torn apart by horrors too unspeakable to believe.

There is a story told of a woman who was walking along a street one day and saw a little girl bare-foot, hungry and cold. The woman said to God "Lord, how can you see this poor child suffer like this and do nothing about it?" The Lord replied: "I have already done something about it - I created you".

This is the story of one of God's creations, Carole Wiley, from Carrigaline, married, four children, an everyday housewife.

Tom Keith
April 1994

PROLOGUE

Despite the warnings of friends and family that it is not yet safe to go to Central Europe after the fallout from Chernobyl, here she is in the broiling heat of the Balkans, sitting outside the simple house of the Visionary Vicka, who has claimed to have seen and spoken with the Mother of God on many occasions here in Medjugorje.

A large crowd has gathered to hear the visionary, and as usual Vicka stands on the steps leading to her front door, the better to see the people to whom she is speaking and the better to be heard by the several hundred of many nationalities who will listen to what she has to say.

The May sunshine has driven the temperatures close to 30°C and being three months pregnant is less than helpful. It is for that very reason that she is here.

It has been a difficult pregnancy and if she were honest about it, she would say that it was unwise to be pregnant at all. But God's will be done and she has heard about Medjugorje and the peace and contentment to be experienced by all who go there.

Even the most hardened and sceptical are seen to soften as the peace and tranquillity make their mark, and many have had their lives transformed by even a short visit there.

Once more she draws her mind back to why she is here. She wants this baby to be perfect and prays with all the fervour at her command that he or she will be born healthy.

If the worst comes to the worst and she dies in childbirth or before, a possibility which is all too real, she prays that those left behind will accept it, cope with it and get on with their lives.

Her requests might be great, but they are simple, and her week in this new village of pilgrimage is filled with heartfelt prayer. Vicka talks of the destination of the soul, the three options, heaven, hell and purgatory and it is the latter which attracts the attention of the pilgrims most.

She finishes her homily, leaves her seat and makes her way through the crowd. The biblical word multitude is particularly apt and better conveys the concept of many people assembled to hear the word of God, even through the second-hand words which come from the lips of the middle European interpreter.

Vicka, the chatty one, makes straight for the pregnant Irishwoman, smiles at her and kisses here on the cheek. Wild thoughts surge through the Irish mother as her heart pounds with dread. I'm going to die, the baby will die, the baby will be deformed.

Her hand goes to her cheek and oddly she thinks, "I'll never wash my face again". She is confused and troubled. Her own vision earlier at the tabernacle during mass, together with the disturbing thoughts of the souls trapped in purgatory have confused her and now as well as all of that she is singled out for special treatment by a young girl who converses with the Blessed Virgin daily.

There has to be something wrong, she thinks. I am being prepared for the worst. Six months later on 3rd December 1986 Kristian Anthony is born to Carole and Tony Wiley, as healthy a bundle of joy as anyone could wish for. Everyone is delighted, the celebrations are hectic and lengthy but Carole cannot convince herself that she has not been chosen for some special purpose.

*****   *****

The phone has been quiet all day with just a call from her younger sister Hillary who wants to chat. It reminds her to contact her other sister Michelle, who is married in Germany, to finalise the arrangements for the summer holidays. Thought of Michelle brings to mind Carole's god-child Jacqueline whose birthday is near and which Carole does not want to forget. Carole is in a world of her own as she prepares lunch. Tony is out with the boys and Sarah and Audrey are playing in Sarah's room.

Like the majority of children, the young Wileys have their likes and dislikes at the table, but this is one dish which attracts everyone.

She hums a few bars of the Robin Hood theme "Everything I do" as she prepares the meal and the jangle of the wall mounted phone brings her quickly back to the present.

Even as she crosses the room to answer it, she has a strange feeling about the impending call but she can not know, that if she responds, life will never by the same again. "Hi Carole" comes the clear Galway lilt down the receiver, but this time there is tension in the voice and it is clear that something is wrong.

Áine Burke, the Galway Garda has been in Medjugorje for three years working with the local people there and looking after Irish groups who come out on pilgrimage.

Her boyfriend Toni is from Mostar and war has been raging in his country for some time. Carole stifles her fears and greets Áine.

Direct as usual, the flame-haired Maureen O'Hara lookalike comes straight to the point.

"Carole, they're desperate for medical supplies out here, everything they have is nearly gone. They're even out of anaesthetics and they're operating on children in their full consciousness. You must do something. You must get supplies. Come out with them yourself if you have to".

Carole's blood runs cold at the thought that such things could happen in a reasonably well-off country on the brink of the twenty-first century. True, they are at war, and hadn't made great advances under communist rule, but the thought of operations without anaesthetics and painkillers is too horrible to contemplate.

She imagines her own children in such a position but cannot come to terms with the reality.

She is aware that Áine is still talking; begging her to do something for the children. Surely there must be people in Ireland who would help.

Suddenly the enormity of it all dawns on Carole. She touches her cheek, the cheek which Vicka kissed just five years before, on a sultry afternoon in a little village which was a part of heaven on earth.

Like a great light being lit, realisation dawns on Carole and she knows what she must do.

Áine is still talking, asking what can be done. Her mind made up, Carole cuts across the voluble Irish girl.

"Give me a list of what you need" she says simply. The Áine and Carole help line is formed.

1

CHOSEN TO SERVE

Since 24th June, 1981, six young Yugoslav children have, it is claimed, been seeing apparitions of the Blessed Virgin and receiving messages from her on a daily basis.

The story of these young people would - and has - made a subject for several books. Mention of Medjugorje draws a variety of comment from people ranging from the sacrilegious through sceptical to the positive and not all those who have travelled to this remote Balkan village are always convinced of the supernatural. .

However few of them who travel either as pilgrims or holidaymakers fail to be impressed with the feeling of contentment and resignation which invariably descends on one at some stage through the visit.

For those who anticipate it, expect it and positively look forward to it, it comes early but the more sceptical and resisting, and those who carry hurt, may have to wait a little longer.

The life of the villagers in the early days of the apparitions was a simple one of farming, reminiscent of Ireland in the thirties and forties.

However instead of potatoes, barley and sugar beet, their crops are tobacco and the grape, both of which could make the country very rich and probably will when the war is over and stability returns.

Forty years of communism and the repressive rule of Tito may have kept the six republics together - they could hardly be described as united - but as in other Communist countries there was little incentive to produce more than just the minimum necessary.

It was a patriarchal society and it could come as a shock to visitors to see the women make their way to the fields each morning to do the days work of tending the grapes or tobacco while the men sat in the shade, smoked, and discussed the problems of the day.

Homes in the village were generally of two kinds. The older house, usually of stone and of very basic rural style, accommodated most of the families; but gradually as more and more pilgrims started to arrive, more and more new houses with all modern conveniences were built in the Medjugorje area.

Some were built with a high level of State help, and what the pilgrims paid for lodgings helped with repayments.

In the early days of the apparitions pilgrims would arrive to find very basic conditions and would be advised to supplement the local supplies with groceries from home.

Very often people were accommodated in family beds inside the home, and even out-buildings were used when necessary.

The state was actively hostile to the visionaries, their village followers and the early pilgrims, but they soon realised that the money the foreigners brought was helpful to the economy and foreign exchange.

The local people made little or nothing from the visitors as the state took as much as possible, and there was barely enough left for people to cater for their guests.

At that time it was unlawful for people to profess or practice their religion openly and people became quite adept at dodging the soldiers' attention, at having furtive prayer meetings and of course, going to the Hill of Apparitions for the daily visit and message of the Blessed Virgin. Here in Yugoslavia you kept your beliefs to yourself, you kept your prayers, masses and worship in the mosques, churches, temples and in your house, but you did not bring it out on the street. That applied to all religions and in the eyes of the law it would have upset a very delicate balance to see one religion enjoy a higher public profile than another.

Here though were the Catholic people coming to the village in droves and openly proclaiming that The Virgin Mary was appearing there.

Many were arrested, ill-treated and generally discouraged from public pronouncement. The Visionaries were regularly chased as the police and soldiers tried to arrest them, and vicious dogs were left loose on Apparition Hill to attack the people assembling there. But still the people kept coming.

Police and soldiers in plain clothes mixed with the crowds, noticing everything, noting everything, and they very often used cameras both to record what they saw and as a further form of intimidation.

Dominating the village is a huge twin towered church built by the Franciscans as a parish church. It is just one of the many parishes which the order serves in the former Yugoslavia and their dedication has made them very well liked and respected among the people.

In the words of one of the locals, when the Turks came four hundred years ago, everyone else ran away except the Franciscans and they have been there ever since. Their service to the people has been dedicated and it continues to be, to this day.

Over the years many people had wondered why such a large church had been built as it could never be anticipated that a town like Medjugorje would ever have enough people to fill it.

It is a belief of the people that this was as much of a sign that something would happen which would draw in the crowds, as any verbal prophecy. So it came as little surprise in 1981 when the news broke that the Virgin Mary was appearing there.

An early protector of the children was Fr. Jozo Zovko, a Franciscan and the then parish priest of Medjugorje, who in the eyes of many has reached almost saintly status.

Foremost among those who admire and respect him is Carole who is greatly impressed by his piety, his sincerity and his

The Church of Medjugorje resplendant in the early morning sunshine

The magnificent church of Medjugorje with its readily identifiable twin steeples. A large dome was added some years ago to accommodate a huge number of concelebrating priests

wisdom, and she is convinced that his role in the village and in the lives of the children is a special one.

In his youth he suffered because of his desire to join the priesthood and the years he was at college were difficult. But his perseverance was worthwhile not only for himself but for all who now hear him speak.

People sit for hours, listening to his every word and touched by his gentle teaching. He portrays the very essence and the very nature of Christianity.

For Carole, his understanding of Christ and the Holy Spirit, and what he portrays Jesus to be, is exemplary. It is a beautiful and uplifting influence for those who listen to him and for Carole there is no stronger witness to the message of Christ than this saintly man from Medjugorje.

Part of that serenity he shared with her on that first visit to his town, a memory which is still clear in her mind and warm in her heart. For Carole it is what she feels life must have been like in the time of Jesus, with his disciples around him enthralled by His every word. Here in the dusty grounds of the church of Tihaljina the people sit around as they must have done on the hills and lakeside of Judea to hear the words of the first Christian teacher.

Fr. Jozo was the perfect pastor to take charge of the difficult task of dealing with such a controversial and demanding occurrence in that remote parish, a choice Carole feels was anything but random.

He was away for the first few days of the apparitions and he returned to find the whole parish in upheaval. There was talk of apparitions, and as he knew the young people concerned he immediately interviewed them at length.

At mass he told the people that if Mary were appearing there, it was in an effort to bring them to Jesus. "Jesus is here in the tabernacle" he told them "do not go on the mountain bringing trouble on yourselves and the village, stay in the Church and we will pray together".

He left to change his vestments and to his dismay when he came out on the altar once more the Church was empty. Everyone had left for Apparition Hill and he was concerned and upset.

He sat in the third seat on the left hand side of the Church and prayed for guidance. Here was a problem of enormous proportions and he needed help. There was only one source of wisdom and comfort and he beseeched Heaven for assistance. "You guided Moses in the desert", he prayed, "give me guidance now when I need it most".

Suddenly from the tabernacle he heard a voice which said "Go and protect the children and I will tell you what to do".

On the mountain as the time had approached for Mary to appear to them, the police and soldiers had come to arrest the children. Under cover of the crowd they left the mountain and ran for the safety of the church arriving just as Fr. Jozo was leaving his seat to go to look for them.

The children came rushing towards him shouting, "Protect us Father, the soldiers are after us", the exact words he had heard from the tabernacle just minutes before. He ushered them into the Rectory for safety and spoke to them about their experiences. He was impressed with their sincerity and believed what they told him.

During the week following, as Fr. Jozo said mass, he says Mary appeared to him, and he has pointed out the exact spot in the church where the cloud appeared enclosing the Virgin.

He can describe her clothing in detail and has vivid memories of her appearances. This is another reason why he believes the children and his recollection of the apparitions is similar to theirs.

According to the authorities he should have stamped out "that nonsense", closed his church, discouraged the children and sent away the visitors. He did not, and was taken to prison where he was subjected to a very harsh regime.

He was beaten regularly and tortured and bears scars of his incarceration including partial deafness since then.

He acknowledges that "they know how to torture" but says it is important to be true to the faith and strong for what you believe.

His congregation became worried for his welfare and one day Vicka asked Our Lady to protect him. That evening during the apparition they were given sight of him kneeling in his cell praying. Mary told the children "Do not worry for Fr. Jozo, for when his time comes he will be one of the great saints in Heaven".

He says that his most frequent visitor when he was in prison was The Blessed Virgin who came regularly and prayed with him for his spirituality and for the trials he would yet have to suffer and to break the chains of Satan around him.

He was sentenced to three years imprisonment but was released after a year and a half. The authorities had begun to realise that events in Medjugorje could be economically profitable for the State and that Fr. Jozo would be a central figure to them. Additionally, there was intense international pressure to release him, so when it eventually suited them, the authorities set him free.

It was a condition of his release that he would not be a serving priest in Medjugorje again and that his passport be confiscated.

He was later moved to Tihaljina where he concentrated on prayer before the crucifix and picture of Our Lady. For hours he would pray with arms outstretched for the people of his country. From early morning to late at night there would be prayer, mass, devotion before the Blessed Sacrament, and meeting with pilgrims.

Whether he had any foreknowledge of what was to come is not known, but he knew in those years that there was much to pray for, and perhaps many have regretted since that they did not join him with their prayers too.

It was against this background that Carole first arrived in Medjugorje as a pilgrim. Like many others who went there, or to

Lourdes, Fatima, Knock or any of the Marian Shrines, she had favours to ask for.

Like the ten lepers in the Bible few enough go back to Medjugorje to give thanks for favours granted but many who do, return time after time seeking and finding that peace and serenity which became their gift when they had asked for the things of the world. But often it was discovered that the gifts they were given were of greater value than those which they had sought.

Carole was a little nervous as the plane dipped down over the mountains on its way in to Split Airport. The beautiful panorama of the Adriatic is a breathless sight and if it were many another country she could savour the breathtaking view, the shining sun, and the beautiful countryside.

But this was Yugoslavia and while it was not an altogether hostile Communist country she knew she would have to act with the same reserve and take the same precautions as everyone else.

There had been stories of those who had chosen to make their views known and a spell in prison with regular beatings had soon changed their attitude.

The people were friendly and welcoming and if their homes were somewhat spartan, the warmth of their welcome made up for any physical hardship.

Generally speaking, the authorities did not want any visitors, but they brought in much needed foreign currency and on that basis had to be tolerated. In the early days, the government gave loans to the people to build new houses to take advantage of the crowds who were coming to the town and of course those loans had to be repaid with interest.

But passports had to be surrendered and it was known which visitors were allocated to each house. Of the amount which was paid by each pilgrim, only a small portion could be retained by the host family while the rest found its way through the bureaucratic system to the Serb - dominated government in Belgrade.

Everywhere one is made painfully aware of the communist rule which held Yugoslavia together for nearly half a century and the man who ruled the country with an iron fist. Even on the road from Split to Medjugorje, there is a huge slogan carved in the mountainside. TITO, VOLIMO TE it proclaims proudly. Tito we love you , the sign if not the people said, but he had guaranteed a kind of stability, albeit at a huge price after his death.

The show of force, subtle though it might have been, was frightening, particularly for the newcomer, but after a while, like everything else, it was treated as commonplace, something to be considered but not feared.

Compared with what she would see in later years, these experiences were quite mild but they were enough to demonstrate the ground rules in old Yugoslavia.

Soldiers and police were everywhere and were noticeably eavesdropping on conversations. Pilgrims would in their excitement talk about the spinning sun or other phenomena they had seen and point to the sky or the mountains.

Often, near midnight, under cover of darkness and to take advantage of the relative cool, pilgrims would climb Apparition Hill by the light of their torches.

When they would hear the aircraft coming they would put out their lights for fear of attracting attention and while there would be few repercussions for the visitor, the host family would be held responsible for this breach of regulations. Spotlights would be trained on the pilgrims from the helicopters to identify them and later they would chastise the people with whom they were staying for not dissuading this conduct.

The guides got to know the particular restaurants which the army favoured and pilgrims would be advised to eat elsewhere. Likewise on the mountain when soldiers would mingle in plain clothes with the pilgrims, the guides would caution the pilgrims against blatant breaches of the rules of their game.

Being three months pregnant on that first trip, Carole had her own difficulties to cope with those first few days. The travelling had taken its toll and there was the morning sickness as well, so she rested frequently and went to bed periodically during the day.

Pilgrims from one of Carole's groups on Apparition Hill

A view of Medjugorje from Apparition Hill.
The Hill is known locally as PODBRDO

The second day, her migraine had cleared sufficiently for her to consider climbing Apparition Hill. Not knowing quite what to expect she set out with the rest of the pilgrims and followed the rough stony path to the top.

She was nearly exhausted when she arrived but immediately a sense of peace descended on her. There is a feeling there which no one can explain but the experience is worth every mile of the flight, every stumble on the stony climb and every thorn for those who go barefoot.

This is where the Visionaries first saw the ball of light which they followed to the top of the mountains. A Lady appeared from the light. Frightened they ran away only to return that evening to discover the ball of light still on the mountain top.

Again the Lady appeared from the light and spoke to them confirming that she was the Virgin Mary and should be known as Our Lady Queen of Peace.

Carole and her fellow pilgrims joined in the rosary, said their own prayers, and came back down the mountain for lunch. They could not wait to return and after dinner took their torches and went back up the hill, stumbling along, hoping not to do themselves serious injury.

They sat by the Cross and about midnight, two of the Visionaries Marija and Ivan, joined them on the summit. They seemed to float over the ground and despite the rough terrain, seemed to come at great speed.

As they reached the front of the group, they dropped spontaneously to their knees oblivious of the sharp stones on which they landed. They maintained their gaze upwards and commenced a conversation with an unseen respondent.

After it was over, they got to their feet, blessed themselves and they were gone. Carole was confused at what she had seen, but over the years since, she has climbed the mountain many times, experiencing that same sense of peace as she did that night.

As they came down the mountain, the little group was assailed by the dreadful barking of many dogs and was frightened by the noise. Despite it being only about one a.m., the birds joined in and the combined noise was very frightening.

The children claim the Blessed Virgin summons them at all times of the night and they come to pray. Sometimes she would call them from their sleep to bring them to the mountain for a message or for prayer for peace, and always they would go.

"Pray that war will be prevented" she has asked and it now seems that she might have been referring to the conflict which was to come and which has shattered the former Yugoslavia.

Carole feels that we now have the object of Our Lady's warnings on the doorstep of Medjugorje, but that even now further bloodshed and suffering can be averted through concerted prayer.

The following day, Carole joined the other English speaking pilgrims for a mass in their own language in the church. In those days there were few enough English speakers around, while there were many Italians and pilgrims from all round the world, in the village.

It is still vividly real for Carole as she recalls arriving for that ten o'clock mass through the beautiful morning Mediterranean sunshine. She took her seat about half way up the church in the left-hand side-aisle.

Mass was fulfilling for Carole who intended receiving Holy Communion as well. She lifted her gaze to see the priest open the tabernacle to take out the Ciboria for Communion.

Suddenly from the tabernacle, there emerged what she is convinced was the face of Jesus. It was in the negative. It was not a picture of a face, it was not an actual face. The closest Carole can get in her description is that it resembled the face depicted on the Shroud of Turin.

The thorns on His head were not represented as the usual wreath, but rather as a bunch atop the head with long spikes and streaks of blood on the face, represented in reverse colour. Only the face was visible with no further part of the body in evidence.

Carole was so taken aback that she did not fall to her knees in adoration. She was amazed, excited but not dumb-struck.

She grabbed the girl beside her by the arm and shook her, still with her eyes on the tabernacle and she asked her if she could see anything. The girl was more taken aback than Carole was as she had to cope with the Irishwoman clutching her by the arm, shouting something about the tabernacle. Those around her could see nothing and when she calmed she went up to receive the Host.

For the first time in her life Carole finally realised the significance of what she was receiving on her tongue and she cried. She had never had this feeling of closeness to Jesus before and her happiness knew no bounds.

She stayed in private adoration for a long while after Mass and when she emerged from the church she was approached by another woman who had been present too.

"What did you see" she asked Carole, but Carole wanted confirmation of what she herself had seen. "Tell me what you saw" she asked the woman who then gave her an accurate description of what Carole had seen too.

She was overjoyed and felt like throwing her arms around her. I'm not mad she thought, someone else has seen it too. All day the feeling stayed with her and in the afternoon she went to see the Visionary Vicka at her home.

She was still full of excitement as she approached the house in the beautiful May sunshine. As usual Vicka stood on the steps in front of her house and addressed the crowd through an interpreter. Carole was "high" on the Holy Spirit as Vicka spoke about heaven, hell and purgatory.

Compared to her descriptions of heaven and hell, Vicka's description of purgatory took Carole aback and suddenly the cloud on which she was floating sank to the ground.

All of a sudden she felt frightened for the souls whom Vicka had described as being in a big dark open space, where there was only one flicker of light in the distance. Amid the wailing and crying, the souls were pushing against each other as they sought to move towards the light which is heaven.

But the souls could not get to the light on their own and were dependant on those on earth to help them there. Every prayer, sacrifice or penance carried out by someone on earth for the souls in Purgatory brought them closer to the light.

"Please do what you can for the Holy Souls", asked Vicka, "they are sometimes the forgotten ones". So every day she has spent in Medjugorje since, Carole has climbed both Apparition Hill and Mt. Krizevac in her bare feet for the Holy Souls.

On one such occasion when she was accompanied by her parents she collected so many thorns the she had to lie on the bed while her mother and father worked on her feet with tweezers.

Vicka had asked that people keep the Holy Souls in their prayers and that is what Carole has done ever since. Remembering particularly relatives and friends who had passed away and people she might have hurt during her life.

When she had finished speaking, Vicka came through the crowd and kissed Carole on the cheek. Carole was alternately frightened and curious to know what it meant and is quite convinced that at that moment Our Blessed Lady had selected her to bring some comfort and solace to the people in Bosnia in the harsh years ahead.

This is not for any egotistical reasons or delusions of greatness, rather an acceptance of a role which was offered and accepted and which she would equally have been free to refuse.

She had more than her share of memories, had had more awakenings than she felt entitled to as she descended on to Irish soil at the end of her trip.

Her mind was still racing with thoughts of the happenings there, her heart still tuned to the spiritual freedom in which she had rejoiced and revelled during her week away. She thought of the hours she had had for quiet contemplation and silent adoration in the church, on the mountain and in the open spaces of Medjugorje.

Now her time was spent at home and she missed the freedom to go to the Church during the day. Worst of all, when she was free at night, the church was closed, something which saddened her greatly.

Whereas, in the spiritual atmosphere of Medjugorje, there were devotions at 10 p.m. or access to the church at midnight, she now felt confined by the Irish traditions.

But there was the baby to plan for, three eternally hungry children and a devoted husband who looked forward to the baby as much as she did.

Out of the blue a phone call arrived asking her is she would organise a pilgrimage and there was no way she could, or wanted to, refuse. Largely pregnant though she was, with the help of Tony and his mother she assembled a full charter group of one hundred and thirty.

Late into the night, the three turned several boxes of tickets, labels and literature into travel packs for their pilgrims and the following day met them all on their way to the airport.

There was no way she herself could go and she was disappointed. There were other leaders to look after them en route to, and in, Medjugorje and they had an enjoyable and fruitful trip.

Carole met them on their return, and realising that she had enjoyed the planning and organising decided that it was something she would like to do again. As well, the guides had not covered all the aspects of a visit to Medjugorje which Carole had enjoyed and she knew that if she were to organise another group she would look after them herself.

She would treat them to spiritual Medjugorje, not just a holiday in a town with a holy shrine. They would do it in spiritual style.

Kristian arrived on time an in perfect health in December. Kristian was Tony's choice of name. Carole had come down in favour of Ethan which has biblical origins, if it were a boy and Megan for a girl. A priest friend who visited her in hospital pleaded with her not to name him Ethan as he would undoubtedly be known in school as E.T.

She contented herself with knowing that Kristian is Swedish for Christian and she was finally happy with the name. Though whether Kris Kristofferson ever finds out that he has an Irish namesake she will never know.

Nine months after Kristian arrived Carole was back in hospital. When she left two weeks later she knew she would have no more children. She was lucky to be alive and she thanked God for her four healthy children and a good husband in Tony.

During an especially joyful Christmas, her memories of prayerful days and contemplative evenings on the slopes of Mt. Krizevac came flooding back to her. She thought again of the sunsets viewed from Apparition Hill, with the gentle sound of Marian Hymn carried softly on the evening breeze. If there was ever a little bit of heaven on earth, this was it and neither army, police nor bureaucratic interference could spoil her vision of their land.

She must get back she decided, and resolved to organise a group as soon as possible, in the new pilgrimage season. For the moment however it was a happy peaceful Christmas with Tony, Sarah, Mark and Audrey, who doted over their new arrival.

2

CAROLE WILEY

There was never anything predictable about Carole Miriam Louise Owens, and even her arrival into this world was a matter of some surprise. Not that she was not expected for she was eagerly awaited like the other five Owens children, but she chose to make her debut in the middle of the night in her grandmother's bed in Cork, on 19th December, somewhat unannounced.

Calling her Carole was an acknowledgement of the Christmas season in which she was born, Miriam was for the Blessed Virgin, the proper form of her name, and Louise she inherited from her both grandmothers.

However she was readily welcomed into the Owens and Bennett household as the third of what would be a family of six children, Declan, Carole, Gerard, Michelle, Hillary and John who died in infancy.

She remembers nothing of her early days in Cork, her family having moved to Dublin when she was just an infant. Her father worked for Fords in Cork but in the 'fifties moved to take up a better position in the Dublin motor firm of Lincoln and Nolan.

Life in the fifties was not easy for most families in Ireland but the Owens were reasonably well insulated by virtue of Mr. Owens steady employment and the practical thriftiness and organisation of Carole's mother Phil.

They owned their own house in the suburb of Clondalkin or at least owned it inasmuch as anyone who had taken out what was then a substantial mortgage could be said to own their own home.

Carole's Mother Philomena who had worked as a buyer with Dunne's Stores was a skilled amateur dressmaker and in Carole's own memory very gifted with her hands. There was no item of clothing she could not make. While Carole had the first wearing of what she made for the family, she also inherited many of her aunts' clothes as well. These were the lean fifties and sixties and Mrs. Owens' skill meant a better turnover of new clothes than in the average household, though not always for Carole.

It was a relief to her when she finally began to earn her own money and she ploughed a good portion of her income into a new wardrobe.

However Mrs. Owens was skilled at many crafts including embroidery, crochet, lace-making, shell pictures and she even did some painting in whatever spare time she had. The results of her work were visible all over the house, but no more obvious than in the clothes which her children wore.

She was a good manager, using the family income wisely, caring for her husband and children and ensuring the welfare of all her charges.

There is no doubt that Carole learned much from her mother and inherited her ability to keep many different strands of life running smoothly.

Neither of her parents drank and the only "vice" between them was her father's smoking which he later gave up. They rarely went out and when they did the children sometimes took advantage of their absence of a kind which still happens in homes today when children are in the charge of a baby-sitter.

One of Carole's earliest memories is of such an evening around Christmas when she was about six. Her father never refused to do a turn for anyone and made many friends. Being a smoker he was often given a present of cigarettes which he stored high in the hotpress to keep them fresh.

Usually they were Sweet Afton and came in flat tins of fifty or a hundred. Later the tins would be coveted by each of the children for a variety of uses, but they were most in demand as a pencil case.

The hotpress was in the kitchen beside the sink and that particular night Carole decided to do her father a favour and count his cigarettes. The baby-sitter had left about ten o'clock so she decided to enlist the help of her brother Declan, the oldest of the family.

They counted the contents of the first box and were delighted with the progress they were making. Carole reached for the second box and as she removed it, it fell from her hand, bounced on the draining board, opened and spilled its contents into the basin in the sink.

The children were horrified, and even though there was only a little water in the basin the cigarettes were ruined.

When her parents returned, they were equally horrified and nothing would convince their father that they were not trying to smoke. No amount of explaining would move him and the following few minutes Carole would remember to this day.

Suffice it to say that they never tried to count the cigarettes again, but it didn't stop her taking up smoking when she started to earn her own money.

Even to this day she has not been able to convince her father of the honesty of her intent and she remembers the incident as much for the fact that she was the leader of the escapade as for the punishment they received.

However, in the way of many incidents which seemed major at the time, she never held it against her father and they developed a special relationship as she grew up. Now Carole's father is her greatest ally and most practical helper in her campaign. He is the one who is constantly available particularly during the daytime when Tony is at work, to travel with her to meetings, talks and business appointments. She knows that a certain amount of activity and social involvement is good for him, and though often her's is a gruelling schedule he never has difficulty keeping up.

She knows she would be lost without him. His bright company, his sound advice, his quiet, logical, temperate outlook on life is often the foil for her naturally impetuous approach to problems. They make a good team and they have been through a great deal together over the last two years . His management of the warehouse has relieved Carole of much of the responsibility there, and she knows that not only will the stock be safe but it will be tidily stored as well.

Carole first attended Clondalkin National School and she has few memories of her earlier years. Sixth class she remembers with a particular fondness for the kindly, maternal approach to her teacher Miss McMahon.

Carole loved singing, as she does to this day, and Miss McMahon was the first to tell her that she had a good voice. It was a formative time for Carole and Miss McMahon ensured that her girls received proper preparation for the major upheaval of going to secondary school the following year.

She would sometimes stand behind Carole during singing and she would suggest that she have her voice trained. Though Carole never did, she still enjoys singing and some of her most enjoyable moments with Áine in Medjugorje were when they would sing together.

Whether hymns or ballads it was another area in which they had close compatibility.

Miss McMahon's approach was a welcome change from the more dictatorial style of her former teachers. The girls matured under her sensitive and understanding guidance and felt for the first time that they were individuals and not just one of a group.

They were given responsibility and respect and even after so many years Carole can still remember those days with affection and warmth.

Her graduation to the Presentation Secondary School in Clondalkin was eased somewhat by her sixth class experiences and Carole's time there was made memorable by her teacher Mrs. Brady. The Principal, Mother Oliver, was a kindly nun of whom Carole still has warm memories.

Mrs. Brady distinguished herself in the school by being the only teacher to wear the black gown and she had a unique gift for teaching maths and history.

Through her own individual style, the subjects came alive and her pupils had little difficulty in learning. It was not surprising therefore that these were also Carole's favourite subjects.

She liked art too, and though she has not had time since she married to pursue it, she still harbours hopes that when the children are grown up she will spend more time in front of the easel.

Through the example of Mother Oliver, Carole considered taking the veil herself. Her mother was less than approving and told Carole that she would be disappointed if she took that course in her life, and that there must be something wrong with her to even consider it.

Whether or not a convent lost a good nun, will never be known, but Carole's talents were certainly not lost to the church.

She had always been interested in the stories of the various apparition sites and would read all she could find on Lourdes, Fatima and Knock. She was interested too in the everyday life of the Church and through the years took every opportunity to be involved.

For her, miracles happened everyday and not just those which were reported from the Holy Shrines. The miracle of birth, of life itself, of nature, held her in awe and she could appreciate as much the miracle of the opening flower as the restoration of sight to the blind.

But even had the priesthood been available to Carole she would not have taken that direction. She does not agree with the concept of women priests and feels that if Jesus had intended that the priesthood extend to women he would have included at least one woman among the twelve.

Yes, He had many women among His disciples and women played a major role in His teaching and in His life. It was a woman who gave Him birth, a woman who washed His feet with her tears and whose sins He publicly forgave. It was a woman who consoled Him as He made His way to Calvary and to women He first appeared on Easter Morning.

To Carole, not having access to the priesthood should be no limiting factor in what women can achieve and there are many more areas in which they can excel to at least the same level as men and many beyond that.

Coming from someone other than Carole it could be possible to interpret her outlook as subservient, but not many people, women or men, can claim the same independent outlook or achievements as she.

While she would not fully favour the concept of married priests, she would in some circumstances allow for a married priesthood. In her three years of campaigning on behalf of the people of Croatia and Bosnia she has come into contact with many priests whom she has grown to know, admire and respect.

She has learned of their burning ambition to become a priest, their achievements, frustrations and often the loneliness which accompanies their single status.

Not allowing priests to marry she feels has deprived the church of many good servants and feels that it may be time to look at the possibility of a two-tiered system.

Simply, those whose only ambition was to serve the people in a pastoral way in the local church would be allowed to marry, while those who had designs on advancing further in the hierarchy should remain single.

Not only would it allow for the church to have the best of both worlds but it would increase the numbers in the priesthood and embrace those who had taken the choice of leaving the priesthood to marry.

Carole stayed in very close touch with her church and contributed in all the ministries she could.

The lives of the saints fascinated her and even if she never asked them of her parents and teachers she was still plagued with questions. Who were the saints? What did they do? Where did they live? What did they have to do to become saints? Reading stories about the saints often preoccupied her and even if some people through the ages were caught off guard, Carole's family could rely on her to tell them the right things to do.

If ever a beggar came to the door they would have to be given something in case is was Jesus in disguise and testing them. One Christmas week, when Carole was young, amongst hectic seasonal preparations, a man knocked on the door looking for help. Perhaps Mrs. Owens was under particular pressure or detected some undesirable qualities about him, but he was sent away empty-handed.

"I bet that was Jesus" said young Carole, with tears streaming down her cheeks, "and we sent Him away at Christmas". So great did she lobby on his behalf that Mrs. Owens eventually went back to the street to find him to bring Him home for tea. But he had disappeared, probably rescued by some other neighbour but Carole was convinced that Jesus had been sent away from their door. She had always held the view that if someone felt that he needed help badly enough that he should knock on a door, then he was worthy of some donation.

If travellers called and if there were children of her age, Carole would query them about God, and if they went to Mass or knew about the Blessed Virgin. Carole was never reticent in speech, something which is an advantage to her in her work today.

Like many young people of the mid-sixties she became disenchanted with Mass as it was presented in her teenage years. If young people today feel that they invented the phrase "bored with Mass" they are a quarter of a century too late. By the age of fifteen, Carole had stopped going to Mass, at least when she had the opportunity, and often she would leave home on a Sunday morning, bound for the church and never arrive.

These were still the days when women wore scarves or hats to Mass, or if only casually dropping in to a church, a man's handkerchief. She wondered if it were all true, did Jesus live back then, did he say all those things? Then she would be consumed by guilt for questioning and being, as she then considered herself, a disbeliever. Today, it is considered healthy to question, to enquire, to seek answers but not so in the church of Carole's youth.

But, like many young people, this was a passing phase, and as she grew up, so her faith grew stronger and the foundations which were laid in her childhood sustained her through her doubts.

Carole continued to consider entering a convent, and the desire was occasionally very strong. She had seen how happy Mother Oliver and the other sisters had been and how productive their lives were. Though she never did pursue her dream, she continued to consider the possibility right up to marriage, shelving her doubts, wrestling with those thoughts which suggested she was being disloyal to God, and though she feels she might have made a very good nun, she has no regrets at having taken the path she did. Nor, let it be added, have the other five Wiley's who share her household.

Carole made up her mind early that the academic life was not for her, at least not just then, and having decided, put the next phase of her life in train.

She left school as she had decided that she wanted to be a hairdresser. With her family about to return to Cork in weeks, she wanted to be able to say when she arrived there, that she had started her training. This she felt would save her having to start at the very bottom in Cork so she applied for a job with Tommy Knox, a large salon in Henry Street, near Arnotts.

As it transpired, her family stayed another six months in Dublin and she had the benefit of that length of experience. If she couldn't qualify in that time, at least, she thought, I will have graduated from the floor by the time I get to Cork. The less than shy teenager approached her boss after just four or five weeks, told him she wanted to specialise in colour and have as much experience as possible before heading south.

Perhaps recognising a certain determination, Tommy Knox accommodated her and gave her the scope and responsibility she looked for. She didn't disappoint him and in a very short time she had her own clients within the salon, something which normally takes years. She looks back with appreciation and affection at her short time there and the opportunities he gave her to advance. He gave her huge experience in colouring and insisted she also do a term in his beauty salon on the next floor to broaden her experience.

When she finally arrived in Cork she was more than ready for her job with Tony Bernard. She was recruited as an intermediate thus avoiding the trainee drudgery again. Disaster struck when she contracted dermatitis from using the colour chemicals with bare hands and she found herself on the sideline for over a year.

She was heartbroken but got a job with G.T.S. Ltd., the drawing office suppliers and spent a very happy three years there. When she left she resumed her interrupted hairdressing career in a Cork salon and was glad to be back at the job she loved best.

She completed her training with Glemby International, in the then Munster Arcade and managed at still only twenty years of age to open her own salon in Carrigaline. Her father, she remembers, had to complete many of the contracts for her as she had not reached twenty one but she had achieved the goal she had set for herself at fifteen years of age and continued in that business until her second pregnancy.

Shortly after she left Dublin, Carole returned one weekend to visit her friend Patricia O'Brien. The following morning was Friday and as Patricia got ready to leave for work, Carole complained of stomach pains. They were serious enough, and she had experienced them before, to warrant a visit to hospital. Unfortunately, Patricia's parents were away and as the following day was pay-day the girls did not have enough money for a taxi.

The plucky two went down to the local supermarket and successfully borrowed the fare to go to Jervis Street Hospital. Carole left there a week later without her appendix, but in considerably less pain than when she went in. Stomach pains would not bother her again until she was going out with Tony when an examination showed that she was suffering from a tumour. Successive operations over the next seven years would not prevent her having four children, though the records will show that having Audrey and Kristian defied all medical logic.

Having an interest in Marian Shrines brought her as an early pilgrim to Lourdes where she was very impressed with the atmosphere within the Shrine. It was not difficult to see that just paces away was all that was commercial in France, but when she visited the home of Bernadette, saw where she grew up in humble surroundings she better understood the spiritual Lourdes.

If I had lived then, she thought, would I have accepted just as Bernadette did, or would I have been one to say she was making it up? Later her reinforced faith would be strengthened even further in Medjugorje and whatever spiritual crisis she might have experienced was behind her for good.

Social life for the young Carole was not exactly a mad merry-go-round which is why she frequently found herself in the newly-built Badminton Hall in Carrigaline practising her game and keeping an eye on the eligible men. She occasionally came across one of the founding members, a young man called Tony Wiley, but it was not until they found themselves supervising a fund-raising children's disco that any approaches were made.

During the evening, Tony invited her for a dance, and from there they never looked back. After some years of relatively uneventful court-ship including frequent visits to the cinema, occasional dancing, a great deal of walking and even a few visits to the pub, they began to assume that they would eventually be married.

Always a romantic, Carole wished for the traditional proposal. She reminded Tony one Sunday afternoon while walking near St. John's Holy Well outside Carrigaline, that even though they had already bought the house he had never properly proposed to her, There and then, in the mud of the well field , he went down on one knee and to Carole's delight completed the formalities.

A month later, accompanied by Tony's sister Ann and her boyfriend Owen, Carole's brother Declan and his wife Rita they headed for London to buy the ring and celebrate their new status.

They toured six or seven jewellers returning to buy the first ring in the first shop which Carole decided she preferred.

They were married in Our Lady and St. John's Church in Carrigaline before Fr. O'Riordan on 12th August 1978, a day they are not likely to forget. There ensued a tale which Fr. O'Riordan has recounted regularly and often since, and it has become part of the folklore of the town.

The trip to Passage the evening before for the almost mandatory confession turned out to be a damp affair with the torrential rain causing problems for new hairstyles. They were to be married at 10am, early even in those days, so Carole rose at seven to begin her preparations. First weather reports were not encouraging and the sight of a damp, misty morning was sufficiently discouraging for her to contemplate pulling the covers over her head and sending word to Tony that they would try another day.

Standing in her wedding gown, she experienced the usual pre-nuptial doubts and her friend Annette exhorted her to make up her mind once and for all. The thought of Tony, forlorn at the altar removed any lingering doubts and she turned up the permitted few minutes late on the arm of her father.

When they re-emerged after the ceremony the sun was blazing from the heavens and it turned out to be one of the hottest days of the year. So hot in fact that the band decided to play outdoors. Wasps buzzed the guests and several suffered stings. Notwithstanding the weather everyone enjoyed themselves tremendously and as it approached 5pm, Tony's brother Barry suggested they leave to catch the train to Dublin for their flight to Venice the following day.

Being wise and organised, and unflappable under pressure, they ran through their mental check list and discovered they did not have their passports. As was the custom of the time, Carole's passport was made out in her married name, but as she was not entitled to it until after the wedding it was to be retained by the celebrant.

They concluded that by now Fr. O'Riordan would have discovered the passport in his pocket and would probably have gone to meet them at the train station in Cork. Mistake. They arrived at the station, Fr. O'Riordan did not. At this stage Carole had developed a migraine so they went to Frank's house for Carole to rest, and the rest to plan.

There's no need for panic, said Carole, we have until midday tomorrow to be at the airport. She swallowed a fist of aspirin and lay down for an hour. They resumed their search for Fr. O'Riordan, left a message on his answering machine to meet them at the train, headed on to the station and when he had not arrived watched the last train depart for Dublin.

They returned to Carrigaline and when they called to the priests' house, he was just returning from the airport where he naturally had not met them. He had encountered some confusion with the message from the answering machine.

He insisted on driving them to the airport in Cork to see if there was any flight to Dublin. Only an empty plane was returning but as there was no air hostess on board they could not be accommodated. Nothing would do him but to insist on driving the newlyweds, whom he felt he had discommoded greatly, to Dublin himself. He had a brand new car he said and it needed a good run. So the priest sat behind the wheel, Tony took the passenger seat and his bride of some hours contented herself in the back and the happy trio set out for Dublin.

Of the several discomforts of that wedding night drive, Carole's inability to have a cigarette was the greatest. She appreciated Fr. O'Riordan's going out of his way to get them to Dublin but she would naturally have preferred to gaze across a railway carriage at Tony and there would also have been an opportunity to smoke.

They stopped for dinner along the way and approaching midnight Fr. O'Riordan dropped the newlyweds at their hotel. Not unnaturally, their room was gone, but they were eventually fixed up in more humble surroundings. They pressed him to stay but Fr. O'Riordan assured them he would be fine driving back and that he would have a few hours sleep before his Sunday duties.

He took the precaution of arranging a substitute for his masses but a mix-up in the announcement of an anniversary at the 8.30 mass drew an early morning telephone call from a disgruntled parishioner and at that stage he conceded he wouldn't get any rest and reported for duty.

Carole and Tony did get to Venice on schedule, though they noticed for some years that any mention of the Italian city brought a smile to the face of Fr. O'Riordan. At pre-wedding meetings for a long time afterwards, he would advise couples not to forget their passports and he would launch into the story of the Owens/Wiley wedding day.

Venice was beautiful, though if they did not have their own memories, they would remember the trip for the election of Pope John Paul I who had been Patriarch of that city which took place during their time there. They were not long back in Ireland when they were shocked to hear of his sudden death just thirty three days into his Pontificate.

They also met an English couple who had a music store in London. They became friendly and the English people bought a beautiful venetian glass reindeer for Carole and Tony as a memento of their visit. In talking with them they also discovered that they had been the ones to sell Paul McCartney his first guitar and launched what was to become a very successful career in music with some group called the Beatles.

Though she continued her career as a hairdresser after they were married, Carole always seemed to have time to spare to contribute to some good cause. She joined the Legion of Mary and in time became the President of the Carrigaline Praesidium. She enjoyed the spiritual dimension but felt hampered by the fact that she was not allowed to do anything for families she met who needed help.

One particular family in the area were very badly off. Carole wanted to help, and she was advised to have the security and protection of an organisation behind her. She decided she would like to join the St. Vincent de Paul. The organisation had only a short time previously opened their doors to women members but the Carrigaline Conference did not feel they were yet ready to go that far.

However Carole approached their president and offered to join, When he explained that the question of having women members had not been decided she offered them the option of accepting her or having her set up a women's organisation.

They relented, she joined, and for some time contributed to the work of the conference, before the war in Bosnia began to take up all her spare time. She feels a much more contented and complete person since she started work for those organisations and is far happier giving than receiving.

Something else of which she is proud is the Medjugorje prayer group which she set up some years ago. Despite the fact that most of its members - there are just nine or ten - are committed to the campaign too, the group has never failed to meet on a Monday night. They may not all be present, but all the prayers are said, all the intentions included and everyone remembered who should be.

It is a source of some pleasure to the members that they received some years ago a Papal Blessing from John Paul II on their work in Carrigaline.

An epidemic of cholera in Peru in 1991 brought a plea from the religious working there to the people of Carrigaline and Carole helped spearhead the collection of supplies and money. Their first venture, a jumble sale in the local hall raised £700 and brought a grateful response from Fr. Bernard O'Donovan who had worked there and Fr. O'Riordan, who had officiated at her wedding, so many years before.

Carole helped with regular collections of money and goods for Africa and South America so when the call came from Aine to send aid to the people of Bosnia she knew at least where to start. For two years she has laboured day and night on their behalf, sometimes wondering what keeps her going. She does not look for thanks, but knows that the aid is appreciated by the people who benefit from it, and by Dr. Martinovic who uses and administers the medical supplies.

Carole does not court publicity unless it benefits her cause and when she was invited in February 1994 to appear on the Gay Byrne radio show, she saw it as a further means of promoting her work. As happens on so many important occasions, there was a crisis the night before the show. A late night telephone call from Mostar, telling her that a close friend had been shot and wounded, kept her busy until the small hours of the morning. When she eventually retired to bed her sleep was light and fitful and even her drive to the studio next morning was slowed considerably by flooding after long periods of torrential rain.

So it was 9.09 a.m. as she entered the studio for the 9.10 start, and Gay was already playing the familiar signature tune as she sat down across the desk from the man who has held the attention of the nation's housewives each morning for so many years. She was still out of breath as he introduced her on air but she soon settled to his easy style of questioning. They spoke of the war and the need for people to be generous, and she explained that she was just a link in a chain. "Anyone would do what I am doing, if they saw what I saw." she told the nation and the nation's number one broadcaster, and as she described the horrors of the war, the suffering of the people, and the response of the Irish population, one could picture Gay across the desk in his familiar 'chin in hand' pose of concentration.

She explained about containers and their transport across Europe and the huge cost involved, and talked of the generosity of the Irish people, and how they are giving more per head of population than any other country in the world. Carole described the task of aid gathering, the work in the warehouse and her efforts to send balanced consignments containing equal quantities of food, medical supplies and clothes.

She speaks of her visits to schools to talk to the pupils, to fund-raising events and even dances, where she speaks to the people about the horrors of this war.

"And do they listen to you in the middle of the dance?" asks Gay, but he too must have realised at that stage that when Carole speaks of Bosnia with her fire, feeling and passion, even the stones of the road would listen.

The thirty minutes allocated to her go quickly and eventually as Gay begins to wrap up, Carole realises that she has many more things to say, people to mention and events to promote. There is never enough time to do the all the things she wants to do for Bosnia

"You're one formidable woman Carole Wiley, I'll say that for you, and you certainly are organised," said Gay, as he wound up the interview, and the programme jingle severed the link with the audience. As she was ushered from the studio, Gay was making contact with Joe Duffy in Dublin who was part of the rest of the show. Walking to the car she hoped the interview had been a success, that more people now knew of the real horrors of Bosnia, and that her task of filling the next container would be a little easier.

She was delighted to hear a couple of days later that a woman had contacted the show to say that as a result of hearing Carole she had left her tea and toast and had gone out to morning mass to pray for the people of Bosnia and for peace there. After that it was back home, back to her full-time job.

When people ask her what that is, Carole replies that it is the most demanding, least acknowledged job in life, that of mother and housewife. A job where a child is put in one's arms without the benefit of any training, a job which is so often taken for granted with little in the way of acknowledgement. Appreciation yes, but that has to be assumed, thanks too, but that has to be read in the eyes of the sick child. But yet the mother will keep going, the everyday housewife will continue to work and homes all over the world will continue to function.

But there are times when the everyday housewife needs her space. Time for Carole to be with her God, away from the public eye, away even from family. Everyone needs their Apparition

Hill, though few will call it that. Everyone needs to converse with their Maker though not all will acknowledge that.

Amid the hustle and bustle of city life, amid the lesser tensions of the countryside, amid bomb and bullet of the madness of Mostar, there comes a time to make peace with God, and then a time to return to daily life.

A return to the open house and friends calling in, the kettle on the boil and the shoulder to lean on. For those are what matter when all else fails.

To be there for family and friends, a port in a storm, a mooring to attach to, a lifeline to grasp, a haven to come home to, a berth to feel safe in.

All of these are important to Carole, the very reason for her being, the creed by which she lives and she hopes nothing will ever change it.

3

BOSNIA - A LESSON IN REALITY

Carole knows it is going to be a tiring trip and the task of getting the container full, itemised, and all the paperwork complete has been time consuming and mentally draining. She will be away for four days so she tries to plan ahead so that all of the responsibilities will not fall on Tony to keep the family ticking over until her return.

She has laid in extra supplies of food, planned menus and has the freezer well stocked. Not that Tony could not cope, he is well used to administering the family during Carole's trips, just as he used to do when she was in hospital or taking pilgrims to Medjugorje.

This morning he takes her to the airport at 6.30 am for the flight at eight so that all the formalities in regard to the extra luggage she is carrying will be completed on time.

Thank God for friendly airlines she thinks as she struggles with her 34 boxes of hand luggage which the airlines will let her take free of charge.

As they enter the terminal building Eamonn Timmins from the Cork Examiner arrives. He has agreed to accompany Carole to Mostar to experience at first-hand the appalling conditions there.

Carole has got good coverage from the Examiner and they have been very sympathetic to her cause. Eamonn will go as an independent observer and will file several stories in the days he will be there.

Nobody gets off scot-free with Carole Wiley, and Eamonn will have to share the work of carrying the hand-luggage on the way to Mostar, something he does willingly.

He knows it contains a lifeline for many patients in Dr. Martinovic's hospital and that as a result of their efforts many lives will be saved, and endless suffering eliminated.

It is a sobering thought and one which takes much of the weight from the boxes he will carry. Eamonn has been to many of the trouble spots of the world, so for him this is one more assignment of misery. He has learned to build up a defence against what he sees, but one would not be human not to be moved by the suffering of the people.

On the flight Carole briefs Eamonn about what he will find, and tells him of her work with Áine on behalf of the people. The flight is less than an hour and so immersed are they in their discussion that they seem to be only airborne before they are coming down again.

London/Heathrow is not like the homely Cork Airport and they have to be alert to recover all the luggage which will not be transferred directly to the Croatian Airlines flight to Zagreb.

They take trolleys to the carousel and pick up the thirty four boxes, Some of them are extremely heavy being full of x-ray film. The ones containing medicine and syringes are more manageable, but they will all be worth their weight in gold in the hospitals of Mostar.

Carole has assembled virtually all the items on the list sent by Dr. Martinovic and most important are the anaesthetics, painkillers and antibiotics.

They head for the Croatian Airlines desk to pick up their tickets only to find that the courier has been delayed by a crash on the motorway from London.

There is still plenty of time however and it will be another couple of hours before the mid-day take-off of their flight. They adjourn to the cafeteria and continue their discussion of life in present-day Bosnia.

Eamonn has a good reputation as a reporter and he is anxious to understand as much as possible about conditions in Bosnia, the history of Medjugorje and anything which will give him a better insight into his story. He is a man for facts and will want to see first hand what he will write about.

Eventually, when their flight is called the tickets have arrived and they board with the rest of the passengers heading for the war-zone of Europe. There are news people and camera crews, one of whom is English speaking and heading for Tuzla which has been making headlines recently.

Carole thinks to herself that under other circumstances the flight could be an enjoyable prospect as it had been on the many trips she made before the war.

She asks Eamonn about life as a reporter, his girlfriend and talks about her own family back home.

It is only two hours to Zagreb, something which brings home to Carole, how close to Europe this conflict is. Such thoughts turn to bitter mental condemnation of a Europe which has stood by and watched a near neighbour tear itself apart.

Soon, she thinks, Yugoslavia will be a candidate for the E.U. but for the moment is outside the club, out of favour and out of benefit. If governments had done their work properly, if the E.U. had acted with any cohesion and decision she would not now need to be on a mercy mission there.

With a plane-full of pilgrims perhaps, but why should it be left to an everyday housewife who had met and befriended some people in Medjugorje to keep alive their neighbours in the mountains.

The announcement of the impending landing in Zagreb brings her back to reality and she is glad to be on the ground again. She smiles as she remembers their arrival in Zagreb and Split on the last occasion just two weeks ago when she had arrived with Fr. Sean O' Driscoll carrying a huge amount of luggage.

Amongst the boxes they were carrying on that occasion there was one containing two large brown jars filled with liquid, probably a cough mixture which Dr. Martinovic had looked for on his list.

It was an uneventful journey through London to Zagreb although they did notice some confusion or concern as they left the plane to wait in the terminal building at Zagreb. As they returned to the plane to resume their journey to Split they noticed that as the men were loading their luggage, they would walk away from the trolley, wave their hands in front of their faces and grimace. Something obviously smelled very badly.

As they sat in their seats, Fr. Seán by the window and Carole in the middle seat, they looked out to see some of their boxes being taken away. They gestured to the baggage handlers who were removing two boxes which were wet, and Carole wondered if they had been ruined by the rain. It later dawned on her that one of the jars had been broken and had leaked its contents onto the other boxes.

They had little time to do anything about it as the plane prepared for take-off and the air hostess assured Carole that there was no problem, that any items left behind would follow later. Shortly afterwards they landed in Split, recovered their luggage now minus the two boxes left in Zagreb and loaded themselves, three pilgrims for Medjugorje and their baggage onto the minibus which had arrived from Mostar.

On the bus there was a strange smell coming from the boxes which had obviously been splashed with the contents of the broken jar. Soon they were all asleep, but were conscious of the driver stopping several times to refresh himself outside the bus. Several of the passengers got out too, to get relief from the strange smell.

When they reached Medjugorje where they would stay overnight they unloaded their boxes. It was late, Carole was nauseated by the fumes and was desperately tired, so without dinner she went to bed and slept like a baby all night.

At breakfast she was asked if the noise of the shelling or gunfire had kept her awake and she said quite truthfully that she had heard nothing. She checked with the airport but the offending and offensive boxes had not arrived and she concluded that they had been confiscated and had probably ended up in a Zagreb hospital.

When she arrived home she checked with the donor company to see what the contents were and was horrified to find that it was ether. It's leaking on the plane might well have caused either a fire in the hold or the pilot to be overcome, neither of which would have a pleasant outcome and how their bus-driver kept awake on the three hour drive to Medjugorje she will never know. No wonder she had slept so soundly that night.

Ever since then, she has not taken liquids with her on her flights and is content to pack them well in a container where they can do no harm.

The flight to Split on the Adriatic coast will be a short one, but Carole is only too well aware that this is the most dangerous leg. This is Croatian airspace, a war zone which is regularly shelled.

As they circle the airport she can see evidence of the war in the roofless houses, the burned out factories and the military presence on the airfield. Standing on the apron is the huge green aircraft which flew in their airspace just minutes before, checking that it was safe to land.

The thought is at once both comforting and chilling and the final proof that they have arrived in the heart of the trouble-spot of Europe.

As they make their way to the luggage conveyor belt Carole wonders from which side she should approach She chooses badly, for across the baggage the red-haired Áine is waiting to meet her Irish half.

"Wiley it's good to see you", she shouts and with one large bound Áine is across the conveyor and hugging Carole so tightly that it seems as if she wants to touch her very homeland through the new arrivals.

She greets Eamonn almost as warmly, and as they recover the thirty four boxes she tells her visitors just how badly off the hospitals are for these supplies.

Getting the parcels on the trolleys is the easy part, for ahead are the security checks and highway checkpoints.

This is Croatia and the supplies and people are destined for Bosnia/Hercegovina and the guards treat it all with suspicion. However through the network of checks and document inspections, Áine can be of help and she explains about the mercy flight.

Dr. Martinovic had previously arranged for documents for them to explain about the supplies and to request safe-passage, and these help appease the naturally suspicious army and police.

Áine, Carole, Eamonn and their driver, set out on the three hour drive to Medjugorje. Today they have to take a rough country road through the mountains and soon it will be dark. At the many checkpoints the guards peer into the car, demand passports and inspect the English speaking visitors closely.

They say they are going to Medjugorje and this eases the suspicions somewhat. To have declared an interest in Mostar would have demanded more explanations, but the mention of the town of the apparitions is its own explanation. Áine points out the snow on the mountains for it is March and the Spring has only shortly arrived.

They are thoroughly worn out when they reach Medjugorje and after they have a meal all they want is sleep. Carole rings Tony to tell him they have arrived safely and retires to take advantage of as much of the night as possible. The truckfull of supplies despatched from Cork a week before was due tonight but did not arrive. It will have to be dealt with tomorrow.

Feeling much fresher for the nights' sleep Carole and Eamonn are out and about early. They go to the famous twin-towered church for 10am mass, and afterwards she shows him around the village using all her expertise as a guide which she had acquired just a few short years before.

They have coffee after mass and though they don't realise it at the time it will be the last food for them that day.

She climbs Apparition Hill, and afterwards in preparation for the arrival of the truck Carole decides to have a siesta while Eamonn prepares his story for the following day's Cork Examiner.

Carole is cold and gets only a fitful sleep. At 5pm the truck arrives and immediately all answer the summons to help get it unloaded.

They take it to the storeroom and Carole soon finds that her decision to leave the goods on the pallets may not have been a good one. While there were pallet-trucks and forklifts available in Cork, they are non-existent here in Mostar and they settle down for a long evenings work.

There are sacks of potatoes, pallets of tinned food, toilet rolls and nappies and they have to be separated into those destined for the hospital and those which will be taken into the mountains to the little village of Ulog which Áine, Carole and Fr. Seán O'Driscoll found with its inhabitants suffering the rigours of war just two weeks before.

When the container was unloaded in Rotterdam some of the goods were transferred incorrectly to the waiting trucks and this error has to be put right too.

It's obviously going to be a long night and Carole regrets not having stayed for dinner.

Back at the house Eamonn comes down for dinner and sends his story on the telephone link to the Cork Examiner through the wonders of new technology, his laptop computer and the miraculous modem.

Dinner was to be at nine, and by ten Eamonn and his host family decide to go ahead without Carole. The electrical power is coming and going and it is difficult to keep the meal hot.

By eleven they are worried and go out to see if she is coming, but it is unwise to break the curfew even in relatively quiet Medjugorje.

Carole arrives home at 2am and straightaway tumbles into bed in the dark house. She is exhausted from the work, the cold and the tension and despite the fact that she is starving she is asleep in seconds.

The following day Eamonn quizzes her about her whereabouts the night before. Despite his young age he sounds like an overprotective father scolding his daughter for being late home from a dance but he is pleased to see she is safe and reasonably well rested.

Later the little group decides to divide the food into manageable hampers for the families in Ulog. They have no plastic sacks in which to apportion the food for the families in Ulog and their driver is despatched to find some. He is back at seven p.m. and together with Eamonn, Áine and Carole, they divide up the sixty bags of potatoes and the pallets of food into eighty bags, one for each family unit in the village.

It is difficult from an Irish perspective to judge the reaction of the people who would receive the regular truckloads of aid in Bosnia. To say that they would be ecstatic would hardly be an exaggeration, and the people must from time to time have thought about who was sending the welcome lorryloads of goods which arrived so regularly.

How many knew the trucks were filled with material which an everyday housewife in Ireland had coaxed from a sympathetic population, no-one can know, but if they thought at all they would have realisaed that the careful mix of food and medicines and the relatively small quantities of clothes, must have been decided by someone who knew their needs.

In Ulog there were tins of beans, peas, and soup, flour and cooking oil as well as soup powder and toilet rolls to be divided and it took until 3am.

Once more Carole has missed dinner and it is no consolation that the others have too. The women have left an hour before to prepare coffee and Carole looks forward to this luxury.

When she arrives back at the house she finds that instead of just a snack, they have prepared a welcoming meal from their

54

meagre resources. Under other circumstances she might have been conscience-stricken about, eating so much, but Carole was too hungry and tired to consider such niceties..

Some time after 3.30 a.m. they climb back into the trucks which are now ready for their separate journeys to Mostar and Ulog, to return to their house. Carole's travels only yards before it gives up with a wheeze. In front, the tail lights of the other truck disappear in the distance and behind, the lights of the house they have left are going out rapidly.

Their driver sprints back to the house and with whatever help they can enlist, push the truck back to wait for morning. They borrow the car and finally at 5am they arrive home and try to salvage some sleep from the night.

More than once, Carole wonders to herself what she is doing in the pitch-black countryside of Hercegovina, with little understanding of the language, shivering with the cold, a target for snipers when she could be tucked up safely in bed in Carrigaline.

The thought of the families in Ulog is enough to chasten her and she chides herself for being selfish, although she does wish that some of those who murmur about " holidays" when she goes to Bosnia could be there to experience the real conditions.

At dawn they all rise again for the anticipated demanding trip to Ulog and after breakfast their driver arrives with the once more functioning truck.

They take the little road to the village in the mountains and there are refugees along its length outside Medjugorje. They daren't stop or the lorry would be stripped and in any event the people will be well looked after in the village.

The mountain road is in an appalling condition and is extremely narrow. To say that Carole is nervous is an understatement and she concludes that this road is much worse than the one she traversed just two weeks before with Fr. Seán O'Driscoll when they had arrived in Ulog to find the most heartbreaking conditions they, in their limited experience, could imagine.

Carole had thought that she had seen and heard the worst from the residents of Mostar, but this war throws up worse excesses almost daily.

They had known they were coming into a badly hit area as they saw the conditions of the houses. The tell-tale pockmarks of the bullet holes on the outer walls of the houses prepared them for the casualties, and the taped-up windows suggested a population who knew how to deal with shelling and the problem of flying glass.

Ulog hardly merits the title village, rather a cluster of houses clinging precariously to a hillside in the same fashion as the inhabitants cling precariously to life.

No dwelling seemed to be intact, and many carried plastic over their windows in the absence of glass. Several roofs were in the process of being rebuilt with rudimentary materials.

The place had a desperate look about it. Well off in better times, the arrival of the war had taken a dreadful toll. These were people who had enjoyed a comfortable lifestyle, had beautiful houses, well furnished with all the modern conveniences and appliances of today. Overnight they had their enviable lifestyle taken from them and suddenly found themselves with only the clothes in which they stood. Slowly some of the villagers had started to emerge. They had been wary of the strangers when they had arrived but when they had discovered that Fr. Seán was a priest they had opened up to them.

Their tale had been a catalogue of horror since the attacks on their village during the previous year and survival had been a full time occupation through the harsh Balkan winter.

Not only had they had to cope with the harsh physical conditions, but also with the murder of some of the inhabitants by Serb forces. Their story had been a heartrending one of gratuitous killing, an orgy of murder perpetrated on an innocent, remote community minding its own business and not involving itself in the war which had visited their land.

When he returned home Fr. Sean committed to paper the reports which he had heard first hand with the help of an interpreter, and as he listened to his tape recorder in the relative comfort of his study, he could once more picture the horrific conditions they had witnessed. He sent it to The Cork Examiner and other publications to try to let the people know just how bad conditions were in the village. He wrote :-

"**Arrival in the village of Ulog, between Mostar and Sarajevo. Over 70 homes in the village were all totally destroyed by bombing and fires. Most villagers fled as refugees to the coast last year for five months, and when their village was liberated from the Serbs they came back to find that they had nothing. Their homes were burned to the ground by the retreating Serbs. The first family we met were living in the tiny cowhouse which was behind the remains of their former home. The father of the family spoke as he showed us around.**

"**This is the house where we kept the one cow that we owned to supply milk for the family. I was a builder and my family never wanted for anything. Over several generations we had built up our family home here, adding extensions to it. When we came back, after being refugees, we just weren't prepared for what we saw. We couldn't believe things would be so bad. There was nothing left. We killed the cow because it was all we had to eat, and we then moved into where the cow used to live and that is where seven of us sleep now. As I am a builder I was able to fix it up a bit better with some materials I had salvaged. We have lived there since August of last year.**"

"**I pray that in years to come God will give us peace and restore our lives**"

Despite the family being destitute they brought out a few makeshift stools anf offered us coffee. They had a few odd cups, but only one spoon for the whole family. From the little they had they insisted on sharing it. They wanted us to know what happened to them, so that we would tell others and that

Carole inspects the wreckage of a child's motorcar in the ruins of a once fine home in Ulog. The child's grandmother looks sadly on.

Wrecked kitchen appliances in a home in Ulog.

some help would arrive. I was invited to take photos of the destruction caused to their home.

He then went on to show us the little patio space in front of the cowshed which he cemented so that they could have a space to sit down.

The only clothes they had were on their backs. The mother told us how she was given a coat in the winter and as it was too small she made it into a skirt. This was all she had to wear.

"When we came back here we didn't have as much as a spoon to bring with us, no cups, no plates, nothing at all. There was nothing left of the life we knew before. The only way we can survive now is if people bring and give us things. We are a small village tucked away in the mountains and not many people know of our situation. So not many people know we are here. It is not easy to go out and ask because we have always had enough before and it is not in our nature to go begging. So it is only if people come and give us anything that we can survive. Before, we would never have understood the value of a sheet or a saucepan, but it is only when you don't have one, that you realise it.

"When we came back we didn't have any electricity, nor did we have any money either. My sister in law's people brought us the few things we have now. They were able to bring us these few bits from Croatia."

There was another woman, a sister in law, living in the cowhouse too. She told how her house, further down the village, was a total heap of rubble and was the reason she moved up here.

"Down where I lived there is absolutely nothing, not even a cowhouse like there is here", said the woman tearfully.

"Nobody gave us any indication what it would be like. When we came back my nephew came to meet us at the top of the road, and said we should take something for the shock before we came down. But not even that warning could have prepared me for what I saw, not just the destruction of my own home but of all my neighbours' homes too.

In the next house another family came out and asked us to come see where some of the people were shot.

"It was so terrible. We were trying to defend the village from the woods. My father was shot dead down there. He went out with a lot of old people with their hands in the air and the Serbs gunned them all down. The fighting was so bad that we couldn't go down to collect his body for five hours. He was dead by then. When the Serbs surrounded the village I was stranded at this end of the village and for fifteen days I had nothing to eat"

We met an old man who had been taken to a concentration camp for fifty days. He was in tears and couldn't talk about it. Almost all families had suffered bereavements.

Another man told us how they had lived there for generations. "My father, and his father before him, built up the house, and when I got married I added on an extension and made it nice. When our house was bombed we didn't cry, because my father, who was still alive then, said to thank god we escaped with our lives."

His wife continued, "For the fifteen days of the shelling I didn't know if my husband was dead or alive. We were so hungry we brought in grass and boiled it. The men took stalks from the potatoes and smoked then to stay sane. Now we are totally dependant on whatever help comes from outside to survive. Nobody has any food or money, and even if we had money there is nothing to buy here."

Another man said :- "In the early days of the war we used cry about what was going on. We thought we knew war then but we never imagined what would happen to us. How can we even begin to explain that to children?"

"At the back of the village there was a new road being built. It was something we had looked forward to for many years to make the village more accessible. We never imagined we would have the road but not the village ."

"There was a woman who came to visit and asked if she could use the bathroom, without even realising that we couldn't possibly have one. I was so embarrassed, because I couldn't tell her to go and do what we do, and go behind a bush."

"We never have cake or cigarettes or anything." At this point Carole offered half a bar of chocolate to one of the children, a girl of about eight years. She held it in her hand and didn't eat it. We were surprised, until she explained. "I must wait for my brothers and sisters to come and share it with them."

The family showed us a radio, the only way they had of getting news of the war, but they had no batteries to operate it, so they were left cut off from what was happening around them. As they were leaving they showed us the garden where they were beginning to plant some vegetables for the summer. When the Serbs burned their house the heat of the flames was so intense that the fruit trees nearby were scorched and we could still see the burned oranges and fruits on the trees.

There were several other families we met in the same plight. All invited us in to photograph the remains of what were once beautiful homes. They pleaded with us not to forget them. Already since our arrival home on Tuesday the 16th of March, arrangements have been made to ship a forty foot container of food, clothing, utensils and medicines to Rotterdam, en-route for Mostar. Within a week these supplies should reach the villagers of Ulog."

The woman who told them how she had brought in grass and cooked it for the family in an effort to survive, reminded Carole of stories of the famine in Ireland.

Two unnecessary tragedies, millions of casualties in each because of greed. She finds it hard to control her tears, harder still her anger which wells up within her at the thought of these people abandoned by Europe. She recalls an interview she had given the previous Autumn when she had tried to get the message across to people of what was happening in many parts of former Yugoslavia.

People can't say they don't know, she told her interviewer but it made little difference to those with the power. If governments hid their eyes, the ordinary people made up for them in their help for these stricken people.

Carole is brought back to the present by a young girl of seven or eight looking up hopefully into her face. She is pale and gaunt with hair which would be blonde if it could be washed and obviously she has not eaten well for a long time.

She rummages in her bag and finds an open chocolate bar and hands it to the child. She toys with it, reluctant to open and eat it and Carole asks her what is wrong. "I will wait for my brothers and sisters to come and share it with me" she tells them simply and it takes a superhuman effort on Carole's part not to break down there and then. The humility and generosity of this young girl in the midst of her suffering and degradation gave her a dignity which immediately earned Carole's respect.

All the tales of horror, loss and deprivation are there and Carole and Fr. Sean can only promise to come back with supplies in a couple of weeks.

Now as the truck makes its way up the hillside with its load of life-giving, morale boosting supplies she is grateful to the people of Ireland for their generosity and to R.T.E. and the Cork Examiner for the opportunity of making the appeal which brought in the flood of aid and money.

Hours after she had come home she had appeared on the late news on Network 2 and still visibly shaken and very angry she had told of what they had seen.

This time there was a professional reporter with her, but would those with power and the ability to make things better listen to him, any more than they had listened to others

Carole and Áine had been through the corridors of power in Ireland in January and they had got a warm welcome in several ministries. Carole would have liked to have seen more visible action by the Government later, in bringing international pressure to bear on those countries which could have influenced events in Bosnia/Hercegovina. This, she felt was our international strength, to be able to force the world powers to act where we may be too small and weak to do something ourselves. It may have been happening behind diplomatic doors, but our stance should have been more public, she felt.

Here though, was action by the people, she thought as their lorry wheezed up the slope which threatened to thwart their progress every yard. It was little wider than a forestry road back home, and the surface was pitted and potholed. Nothing more than a dirt track really, suitable only for a horse and cart.

Worse still, in places it was a series of hairpins and on Carole's side - the passenger side - there was a sheer drop of hundreds of feet.

So great was the climb that Carole felt one could slip even walking but still the engine wheezed and kept going. She left down the window to clear the fumes and could hear the boom of artillery in the distance.

Their driver identified it as being in the Mostar area, and Carole whispered a prayer for the unfortunates at the receiving end and for Dr. Martinovic who would soon be treating the injured. The supplies she had carried would soon be needed she thought.

On the outskirts, the village has all the appearances of being deserted, but a head appears around a door and soon people are appearing in the street as if by magic.

They select a straight stretch of road in which to stop and Carole hopes the hand-brake is sufficient to the hill. Áine had been here a week before, so they are expected and the villagers come running with a variety of wheelbarrows, prams and even a battered bike to wheel away their supplies.

The hampers are claimed by the villagers as their names are called from Áine's list. It seemed impersonal but there would be chaos otherwise. The boxes of clothes and blankets are left on the side of the road for a lucky dip and there is plenty of activity around them.

Armfuls of jumpers, trousers, shirts and coats are taken away and soon nothing is left. One woman looks curiously dressed to Carole and on close inspection she sees that her skirt is an overcoat which has had the arms and the collar removed. She will appreciate the dresses and skirts from Ireland and again Carole murmurs a thank you for the Irish people.

The villagers had left when the Serbs took over and had been gone five months. They had returned to find not only their houses damaged, but the contents totally destroyed or stolen.

People who had enjoyed a reasonable lifestyle now lived in out-houses which previously had belonged to the farm animals and they were glad of even that shelter.

On their previous visit Carole and Fr. Seán had been invited in to their makeshift homes. On that occasion the people had had nothing to offer them to eat and were visibly embarrassed. Now, with the Irish supplies they could offer coffee and be hospitable again.

Thank God for Irish generosity, Carole thought, for with the little amount of material goods came a resurgence of these peoples' dignity once more.

A woman says to Carole that they have been praying rosaries to Heaven to stop this war. "But Heaven not listen" she concluded sadly.

Carole finds inspiration and tells her that Heaven listened alright and gave Ireland a tap on the shoulder. The woman is touched by the humour and Carole thinks to herself that the people of Ireland must have been Divinely inspired to contribute as they did.

After the supplies have been distributed Carole walks round the village. She meets a woman who is weeping softly, gazing at a child's sit-in car. Carole suspects what is wrong and makes a gentle approach.

The woman is dressed in black shawl and dress, as a traditional Irish widow might have been dressed at the turn of the

All Carole and this Croatian grandmother can find of use in the ruins of her home is a solitary spoon. Her husband, her children and her grandchildren all lost their home when this previously well-equipped house was shelled and destroyed.

Peace my friends . . .
A young boy acknowledges the first humanitarian aid to be brought to
the village of Ulog during the war.

Irish blankets and clothes are welcomed by the local population in Ulog

century. She breaks down completely and sobs in Carole's arms as she tells of her grandchild who had owned the car and who had died in the war. Feeling helpless, all Carole can do is hold her and cry with her.

She tells her of her own children who were shot at they tried to escape to the woods and how the Serbs, when their advance had been successfully halted by the Croats and Muslims fighting together, put the village to the torch and wrecked anything of value. On their retreat the Serbs had destroyed what they could not take, and as Carole searched the debris of one house with it's elderly occupant, all they could find of any use was a solitary spoon. Amongst their many skills, a scorched earth policy came easily to the Serbs.

The woman has few relatives and no possessions left. Words fail Carole and she wonders if there is any end to the sadness which is Bosnia today.

These are people who knew better times, who had good houses built up over generations, who had businesses, workable farms and a good standard of living. Now they are reduced to penury, stripped of even their dignity as they struggle to survive to tell the world of the horrors. But few in the world want to know.

Carole still had one task to perform but she couldn't have envisaged the joy it would bring. On her previous visit, when she had promised to return, an elderly man had asked her through Áine to bring him back a radio. She had managed to get one and a spare supply of batteries, so now the community would not be cut off from the outside world again.

When she produced the radio to him, his eyes lit up like lighthouses on a dark night. Tears poured down his cheeks and he grabbed Carole by the shoulders and hugged her.

Alternately kissing her cheeks and hugging her, she felt the blood drain away from her but he had left her in no doubt as to the value he placed on the item.

She was afraid he would fall to his knees in front of her, but suddenly it was all worth while, the pleading, the wheeling and dealing, the long nights in the car, the long hours in the warehouse, the plane journeys, the cold, the hard work, the dangerous mountain journey.

Now she could actually understand what these everyday things meant to the people, not just the food which would keep them alive, but all the items which had been donated in Ireland.

There were sweets for the children, some biscuits which they had not seen in a long time and how they loved them all. Eamonn Timmins was moved to write in the Cork Examiner about the deprivation he had seen as follows:-

"Ulog, situated on a mountainside between Mostar and Sarajevo, was taken by the Serbs in September 1991, and recaptured by the Croatians in June.

During the last 12 months the villagers have experienced horrific suffering. When the Serbs abandoned the village last June they destroyed all in their wake. Ulog was reduced to a burnt-out shell, with houses torched, water supplies cut and bridges dynamited.

Factory worker Pavo Bikosic (66) was one of 20 elderly men in the village who were rounded up in June and trucked off to a concentration camp in northern Bosnia.

His two-and-a-half months there were a living hell, spent in atrocious conditions. When he was released last August he had lost 50 pounds weight and needed a blood transfusion.

Severely beaten on several occasions, Pavo rolled up his right trouser leg yesterday to reveal horrific bruises. His three front teeth were smashed by a blow with a rifle butt.

Each day was spent in darkness in a former officers' mess which he shared with 24 other prisoners. He also endured psychological torture. The man was told that one of his sons, who was fighting at the front for the Croatians, was dead. This later turned out to be untrue.

He returned to find that his home, like all other buildings in the village, had been destroyed by the retreating Serbian forces."

It was sensitive, emotional but factual and he succeeded in conveying to the people of Ireland the hopelessness felt by the people of Bosnia and their sense of abandonment by the countries of the world.

They said good-bye to the people again and as they came down the mountains, the anger and bitterness once more welled up in Carole. For a moment she was angry at everyone but as the mist in her eyes cleared she realised that her anger was directed now at those who had the power to make all this stop.

They claimed to have the wisdom and knowledge and experience to be in control, she thought, but she doubted that amongst the thousands who enjoyed that status all over Europe there were a handful who really cared.

The precariousness of the road soon took over her thoughts and she envied Eamonn Timmins who had retreated into the closed back of the lorry to put his story together. He was spared the view of the sheer drop, but she knew he had his own battle to fight and ghosts to exorcise as he struggled to put the horrors he had seen and heard in cold print.

She appreciated the support and help he had been on this trip. He too was shocked and exhausted by the events of the last few days and she wondered what words he could find to describe what he had seen and heard. For a while he had been aid-worker and reporter, and she was proud of him and wondered how many others in his position would have been as ready to pitch in.

Now she knew he was a cut above the usual Hilton Hotel war correspondent and willed him to find the right words as she heard the light tap of his word processor behind.

As she tried to imagine how he would write the story, a battered and rusty car appeared in the distance travelling towards them. It looked as if it had taken refuge from the set of a stock-car film with a door missing and it was liberally decorated with bullet holes.

They would meet at an upcoming hairpin and unfortunately, she saw, they would be on the outside. As they pass each other, neither driver wishing to reduce speed, the back wheel of their lorry spins on the edge of the cliff. Carole's heart almost stops an she calls on more than the Holy Spirit to help them in their need.

She firmly believes these are her last moments alive and she is conscious of calling out aloud for absolution for all the past sins of her life.

What she confessed to in those moments she can not remember, but she knows she will never again have such a firm purpose of amendment as she had on that hairpin on the Ulog road.

It is not until they are back on a relatively straight stretch with fences on both sides that she takes her first deep breath and relaxes a little.

Soon they are home safely, and Carole rings Tony to assure him all is well and then, mentally and physically drained she falls into bed for a couple of hours sleep before dinner.

Áine arrives about nine pm and they have dinner with the occasional staccato burst of small arms fire in the distance. Afterwards, they talk for a while, but they are all desperately tired and do not stay up late.

The following morning after mass, they set out for Mostar with the Irish supplies. While the city may be closer to the fighting there are no hairpins or precarious roads to be negotiated. They make good time and Dr. Martinovic is delighted to see them at the hospital.

He has an especially warm welcome for Carole whom he knows has organised his much-needed supplies back in Ireland. He can be even more of a doctor now that he has medicines and some replacement instruments.

He takes Eamonn around the hospital, showing him the empty upstairs rooms where it is now too dangerous to house the patients. He points out the bullet marked walls and the room where the shell scored a direct hit. He still has the shell case as a souvenir, though he would much prefer the room so that he could accommodate more patients.

When Carole is asked about the hospital she likens it to M.A.S.H. the television programme, without the humour. One

The sandbagged windows which make the corridors of the building relatively safe for patients and staff. This is the hospital in which Dr. Mantinovic works.

Representatives of the Confirmation Classes of Morning Star Boys School, Togher Boys School and Turner's Cross Boys School with the medical equipment which the classes purchased with some of their confirmation money. Photo Courtesy Cork Examiner

One of the many damaged places of worship in Mostar. This mosque was further damaged later in the war.

One of the hospitals in Mostar which shows very obvious signs of shell damage.

Services at their most basic. Part of Mostar served by a water tanker which fed its supply to public taps.

Carole Wiley gazes at one of the many bridges blown up by the Serbs.

minute all is quiet and they are tending to patients, the next there is shelling and the fresh casualties start to arrive.

Services are basic at best and the whole hospital now operates in what was the basement service area. Consequently, pipes line the ceiling, cables criss-cross, intermittently bringing power and the walls are badly in need of a fresh coat of paint.

Eamonn remarks to Carole that Dr. Martinovic changes character totally when discussing the war. On other subjects he is bright and happy but when the talk turns to bombs, soldiers and civilian casualties, his face clouds over and he is a different man.

It is over a year since he received a salary. His medical supplies come mainly from Ireland, he has little or no equipment and irregular power supplies.

The only thing he has in abundance are patients supplied by the war and he wonders if there will ever be a normal life again.

On a previous visit he told Carole of the agonising decisions he has had to make in relation to patients and their treatment. He spoke of the occasion when he had to amputate the legs of a little girl because of her terrible injuries. He had no anaesthetic left, so he, and she, had to make do with whiskey.

"No doctor is trained for this" he told Carole and on his face was a pain and sadness which reached into his very soul. He has had to carry out similar operations without even the benefit of whiskey, so when a consignment of medical supplies arrives from Ireland the first thing he checks for is anaesthetic.

It is also a priority for Carole who can readily imagine the terror an operation without the drug can cause. He had told Fr. Sean:

"All of what you brought in the past was what we needed most. I have been using some of the medicine very sparingly. I keep it in my room and anyone using it has to come through me, so not a thing is wasted. Often, when I would be making a list of what's needed for the hospital, I'd have it finished and wouldn't have thought to put down food. But of course we need food to feed the staff and the patients. They all have

been coming to work right throughout the war, although nobody has got paid for the last year and a half. There is no money, so we are totally dependant on aid from outside for ourselves as well as the patients. I haven't earned a penny myself, the only money I got was about thirty five pounds from some people. The staff ask me when they see people like you here bringing medicine, 'Did you ask them for food?', and I say 'no I only asked for medicine.

We saw a little girl in one ward. Some shrapnel had been removed from her back. She was orphaned and was so traumatised that she couldn't say how old she was. The next small girl, about 8 years old was a refugee. She was in hospital for three weeks with leg injuries. She told us that things were better now than they were before. The broken windows in this ward were being patched up by used x-ray film.

It is difficult for us to ask for food, and if people realised that we haven't earned anything in the last 12 months then they should ask themselves 'what are we living on?'. That way we shouldn't have to ask and people might offer us food."

He never asks for anything for himself but in an unguarded moment on the last visit he told Áine he had almost forgotten the taste of cheese. The diet is fairly basic and it is easy to get tired of pasta shells, rice and the oily bread made from the aid supplies they receive.

Carole has brought some processed cheese, which will keep better, but she knows that the local taste is for strong blue and cheddar cheeses. She would love to take out a container load of meat which she knows she could get, but the cost of the refrigerated truck would be prohibitive.

Dr. Martinovic is overwhelmed by the amount of supplies which have arrived, particularly the medical supplies which Carole and Eamonn have lugged across the airports of Europe. They in their turn know that the painkillers are priceless here and that the anaesthetic will save patients the agonies of being operated on in their full consciousness. The discomfort which the boxes caused seems a long way off now and they are sorry there were not more supplies to bring.

It is difficult sometimes to convey just how bad conditions are in Bosnia/Hercegovina and how basic and primitive life has become for people. On one occasion on a visit to Mostar Carole needed to visit the loo. Not seeing any facilities, she held out as long as possible but eventually when she could wait no longer she enquired and was shown to a small room with a toilet in the corner. The problem was that it was on the first floor with two walls missing and on very visible display to the public at large. It was one more proof for Carole, of how much dignity has been stripped from these people that very often the most basic requirements such as going to the toilet can not even be private.

To talk of toilet paper, soap and water is often the ultimate in luxury and daily people fall to the sniper and mortar round as they try to get a supply of water from one of a few stand-pipes, the only water supply in the heart of Mostar.

Carole has brought a special present for the doctor. The pupils of Turners Cross Boys School ,Togher Boys School and Morning Star Boys School in Cork have contributed much of their confirmation money and have bought a diagnostic set and a stethoscope for his use in the hospital. He is overwhelmed by the generous gesture and tells Carole that he is greatly moved and humbled by the children's' generosity and that the instruments will be invaluable in his work and of great benefit to the patients.

She leaves to show Eamonn the streets around the hospital which show the ravages of the war conditions. The front wall of the hospital is shored up with planking and sandbags and is very unsightly but reasonably safe for the patients and staff. The rest of the buildings have glass missing and show signs of shell damage.

The graveyards have long since been filled to capacity and open spaces have been pressed into service for burials.

A beautiful tree-lined boulevard with grass margins between the road and walkway has been turned into a makeshift cemetery. It is a further daily reminder if such is needed that this is a city at war. The people are weary, filled with constant tension and always only seconds away from death by sniper or shell.

On one particular visit, Carole and a small group including a Muslim and Croat soldier stroll through the streets of the city.

Suddenly as they cross an open square a shell is fired from a big gun in the hills above Mostar. There is an eerie few seconds wait, while they wonder where the shell will land and they crouch in anticipation.

They run for cover and Carole has a choice of who to accompany. On impulse she follows the Muslim soldier and they crouch in the street looking for the source of the firing. Her attention is attracted by the huge bayonet her crouching companion has strapped to his back and his handgun by his side which together with the light machine gun he is carrying makes him a well armed ally.

The other soldier gives the group a sharp command for them to follow him.Quickly they run to their car .Their driver slams it into gear and roars down the street heading for the outskirts of the city. Carole is queried about her choice of companion and it is pointed out that being beside a Muslim soldier increased her chances of being fired at as it was he that was the main target. She realises that the sheer size of the man and the cover he would provide together with the huge gun he carried must have been a comfort to her. She marvelled at how quickly she had made her decision under fire.

Some months later the Muslim was shot in the leg but was lucky enough to survive the experience. As they climbed the mountain road to Medjugorje, Aine pointed out the Serb tank positions in the hills which ring Mostar.

So far it is reckoned they have used only about 45% of their capacity and stand ready to obliterate Mostar on a word of command. Many fear they have gas shells, which would wipe out, not only the population of the city, but that of a huge area of the countryside as well.

Carole is conscious of the huge amounts which governments spend annually on the arms race. The seventeen billion dollars per week or two and a half billion dollars per day could be put to such constructive use in doing good, she thinks. The diseases of Africa could be cured, the destitute of the Far East could be housed, the grinding poverty of Latin America could be eliminated with that money and a little good will. She is anti-war, anti-violence but also anti-aggression. On one occasion on her return from Mostar, still shocked and angry at what she had seen she was asked about the topic of the day, the possibility of air-strikes against Serb artillery pounding Sarajevo. She agrees that anything which will stop the senseless slaughter should be tried.

She is disappointed when this is later quoted to her as aggression and she finds it difficult to believe that people cannot see the difference between defence and attack. Perhaps it is just for mischief that they want to embroil her in controversy.

"If any of you has a sheep and it falls into a pit on the Sabbath, will you not take hold of it and lift it out". The hypocrites are alive and well yet.

They rest for a short while before their evening meal. Everyone is quiet tonight at the thought of the parting in the morning but it has also been a hectic four days.

They all seek an early bed and are up again at 2 am to leave for Split Airport an hour later. It is an uneventful three hour journey and Carole is not looking forward to the farewells later.

They promise to keep in touch when telephone and fax lines permit and tearfully the two women who have been through so much, both together and individually, for the sake of the people of former Yugoslavia, say good-bye to each other.

As Carole boards the plane she photographs Áine at the terminal, wondering if she will ever see her alive again.

On the plane Eamonn and Carole discuss the weekend events. They find it difficult to believe that they have lived so much in

A tired Carole is welcomed home from her trip to Bosnia prior to Christmas 1993 by the Lord Mayor of Cork, Cllr. John Murray and Carole's husband Tony.

Carole receives her Person of the Month Award from M. Gubbins Cork Examiner Publication, in recognition of her work for the victims of the war in Mostar and Ulog. L to R: M. Gubbins, A. St. John Owens, Carole and Tony Wiley, Phil Owens, Manus O'Callaghan Southern Advertising. **Photo Courtesy Cork Examiner**

five days, have seen so many different aspects of life, have generated so many memories.

They are both physically exhausted and mentally wrung out and they wonder what it would be like to live in that environment permanently. They are glad to land at Heathrow which represents a return to normality not least because English is the spoken language again.

The welcoming Aer Lingus flight brings them back to Cork and their respective families and homes. Carole bids farewell to Eamonn. They will be in regular touch.

Tony and the children are glad to see Carole home again and are at the airport to meet her. She loves to see the family there, and usually they are the only welcoming committee. On a later occasion however as she arrived home after delivering a consignment of drugs prior to Christmas 1993, Carole was surprised to be accorded celebrity status as she came into the terminal building. Asked to supply a particular drug for the treatment of a fungal infection which affected the breathing of children and had killed a number of the young patients, she decided to fly out with the costly life-saving treatment herself. The previous few weeks had been particularly busy in the warehouse and she had got out four containers in as many weeks. It had been a punishing schedule and she was not looking forward to the trip even though Aine had promised to come to Split to meet her, saving her the three hour journey to Mostar.

Five flights in thirty-seven hours had taken their toll on her energies and her spirits, the biting cold and the knee-deep snow in Zagreb were draining, and meeting and leaving Aine in such conditions had left her a little depressed.

As she walked into the Arrivals Lounge in Cork Airport, the Lord Mayor Cllr. John Murray stepped forward to greet her and welcome her back home. She barely saw Tony, so taken aback and delighted was she with her civic welcome, and in typical fashion, when she had seen the Lord Mayor, had wondered what celebrity he had come to meet.

That night however, Carole was the celebrity, and when he found out that she was coming back from Bosnia, the Lord Mayor had no hesitation in going out to meet her on behalf of the people of Cork, on whom Carole's work reflects so well.

"You are a very brave woman", he told a blushing Carole, "and Cork is proud of you." As they chatted in the lounge, and Carole brought him up to date on events in Bosnia, she was conscious of her flak-jacket which she was still wearing, as it was the easiest method of carrying it. However, the surprise reception was just the tonic she needed to perk up her spirits after a tense and demanding trip. They chatted for a while about her work and the Lord Mayor promised to support her in whatever way he could.

In the car the children want to know what she has brought them and make plans to tell their friends in school about the Lord Mayor coming to meet their mother.

Despite the fact that she is desperately tired, Carole resumes her normal role at home immediately. She has been gone five days and not the scheduled four but it is good to be back to the familiarity of routine, to Tony and the children, to her friends in Carrigaline, to coffee with Jan.

As she looks around her well appointed kitchen she ponders on how lucky the family is, on how lucky the vast majority of Irish families are.

Lord keep us that way she thinks to herself and seeing the photo of Our Lady of Tihaljina on her sideboard says one more prayer for Ireland and Bosnia.

4

FRIENDS ON THE MOUNTAINSIDE

They clicked almost immediately, the chemistry was right, they had much the same outlook on life and both had a good sense of humour. Áine Burke is a Garda from Athenry in Co. Galway whose posting was in McCurtain St. Cork.

Aine had moved to Medjugorje in the winter of 1988, and had lived there prior to the war for two and a half years operating as a tour guide in the village, ministering to the needs of pilgrims particularly from Ireland and the English speaking world.

When the war broke out it was a natural development for her to stay among the people with whom she had become acquainted during her years of work there, to help them through this terrible time in their history.

The outbreak of the Croatian war for independence in 1991 followed by Bosnia's attempt for freedom the same year and the subsequent ravaging of the country changed Áine's role and lifestyle, as it did that of every inhabitant of that unfortunate land.

But she had had made her mark at that stage, had contributed her share and had met and befriended a Cork housewife named Carole Wiley.

For Áine, Carole was a godsend. Not only was she someone who was obviously ideal to share her workload, but she became a good friend as well. When Carole took out her first group, it was a step into the unknown, but she knew what was expected from her by her pilgrims..

She knew what she herself had enjoyed the previous year and was determined to make the pilgrimage as enjoyable and as spiritually satisfying for her group as it had been for herself.

She soon learned that taking responsibility for a group is entirely different to planning one's own day and though she was prepared for a good deal of work it turned out to be an even busier time than she had anticipated.

In addition to daily visits to Apparition Hill and Mt. Krizevac, morning mass, meeting with the visionaries, evening devotions, some time needed to be reserved for private prayer.

As well as all that Carole wanted her pilgrims to meet Fr. Jozo as she felt that any trip to Medjugorje would be incomplete without the experience of meeting one of the central characters of the Medjugorje story. No one she felt, could fail to be moved at meeting him and many of her pilgrims expressed their gratitude later for having been given the opportunity.

On the strictly tourist side, she wanted them to see the waterfall, the old Muslim city of Mostar with its famous single arched bridge. The hobbly bridge, Carole and Áine called it, and to Carole's dismay, it was finally blown up November 1993 cutting off the final important crossing from the Christian side to the Muslim side of the city.

It was a landmark in the city and a feature with which almost every pilgrim to Medjugorje is familiar, though few know that it is reputed to have been built from stone taken from Mostar Cathedral destroyed by the Turks in the days of the Ottoman Empire. Just eighteen miles from Medjugorje, the city of Mostar was always a favourite destination of pilgrims who wandered through markets or browsed in the stalls which lined many of the narrow cobbled streets.

Here pilgrims bought decorative brass and leather goods and haggled and bargained with the stall owners like native middle-easterners. Some took mint tea or cappuccino in the little restaurants and savoured the Eastern atmosphere which

In Happier Times . . .
A tourist browses through the souvenir stalls in a street in Mostar.
Note the chimneys which can be compared to these in the photo below.

A street familiar to pilgrims to Medjugorje. Many pilgrims visited the
Muslim side of Mostar to buy souvenirs and drink coffee in the street-
side cafes. Now all that is left is a heap of rubble. The street overlooks
the Neretva Bridge and river.

pervaded the Muslim quarter and were readily welcomed by the street traders.

Highlight of the trip there, was the visit to the Neretva Bridge to see the young men dive into the river almost a hundred feet below.

There is a long tradition of diving off the bridge dating back several centuries. The story goes, that a Muslim woman was crossing the bridge one day when her yashmak blew off and fluttered down to the river below.

As it is unthinkable for a good Muslim woman to be seen in public without her veil, she was horrified at the loss of hers and wondered what she could do.

A passing Muslim man saw her predicament and without thinking dived off the bridge and recovered her veil. She was so impressed by his good deed and so convinced that anyone who would do such a thing for her without thought for his safety could only be a good husband and treat her with respect, that she readily married him.

Thereafter, when local youths wished to prove their manliness or impress a girl, they too dived off the bridge. In latter times the feat was performed for the money the tourists readily handed over.

On the one occasion several years ago when the local television station decided to televise the spectacle live, the attempt ended in tragedy and the youth was killed.

It was some years before the practice resumed but there was never any attempt later to film the feat for commercial purposes. After the outbreak of war there was little market for such deeds of bravery and even those crossing the bridge became a target of snipers. With the demolition of the bridge a tradition of centuries died and it is one of Carole's hopes that when the war finishes and the people of Bosnia are united again the bridge and the tradition will be restored to their former glory.

This was the programme of events which Carole organised for her Irish Pilgrims, intent on making their stay fruitful and

The famous Neretva bridge between the Christian and Muslim sides of Mostar. Note the canopy erected to deny snipers a clean shot at those crossing the bridge.
The bridge was finally demolished in the winter of 1993

In happier times, a diver prepares to launch himself on the sixty foot dive to the waters below.

enjoyable with happy memories to take home with them to Ireland just as she had done herself.

For Carole it was a long day, for when her group had completed their sightseeing, and had fulfilled their spiritual commitments, she would then meet with Áine to plan for the following day.

This involved not only planning the detail of the itinerary but also providing for the special needs of the pilgrims who were ill with a variety of ailments. All contingencies had to be provided for and it was essential to ensure that each pilgrim had any special medication they might need.

This left little enough time for a personal chat and even sitting on a bus together most of the talk would be of their pilgrims' needs.

It would not be until they met in war torn Zagreb late in 1993 that they would have a real woman to woman exchange about their families, their private lives, their hopes and fears for the future.

Their daily demanding schedule left little time for that in the pilgrimage season, work took all their time. Exhausted Carole would tumble into bed only to be woken by the alarm after what seemed only minutes. She would then present herself to the pilgrims and the round of commitments would start again.

It may have been tough going but it was enjoyable and fulfilling. Seeing the pilgrims happy, was payment enough for Carole and if proof that they had enjoyed the trip were needed it was contained in the letters of thanks which many of them sent on their return.

On her first pilgrimage Carole was sharing a room with a mother and daughter as was the usual form of accommodation there. On that first trip Áine was their guide and she wasted no time in getting the pilgrims to their various destinations. Áine does not dawdle and sets a lively pace climbing the mountain or coming from church or going to the houses of the visionaries.

The usually busy Carole was visibly slowing as the day went on and at night she would fall into bed to sleep, if not the sleep of the just, then the sleep of the exhausted.

One morning when a daytrip to the waterfall was planned she overslept and was enjoying her extra few stolen minutes when Áine strode through the kitchen, into the bedroom calling "Get up, Wiley" and snatched the clothes from the bed. "Wiley would you ever get up" she repeated as Carole peered through sleep glazed eyes at this Granuaille-like figure with a shock of red hair.

But there were few who could impress Carole with their stories of Medjugorje, the apparitions and Fr. Jozo, as much as Áine, and when she spoke, Carole listened intently to every word.

She would speak of what happened to Fr. Jozo, of the visionaries and the tests they went through. Her own personal conviction of the reality of what was happening out there was obvious.

Carole and Áine would sit for hours talking about the events of Medjugorje. They would sit late into the night talking of everything under the sun, refilling their coffee cups often but always the subject would return to Medjugorje. A further bond between the two women was that their husband and boyfriend respectively shared the same name. They would joke about Tony with a Y or and Toni with an I and it was always good for a smile.

They found they had much in common and Carole remembers these nights with much affection. They were good times shared among good friends and very often she feels that the foundations of her work of the last three years were laid during their long summer evenings in Medjugorje.

"Please come back soon", Áine would ask of Carole as she would leave for home with her fellow pilgrims and already Carole's mind would be made up that she should organise another group that year.

They would ring each other regularly across the countries of Europe and renew memories of their days together. When Áine would visit Ireland, time was set aside for a Cork visit and their special friendship blossomed between the women at home too.

They grew to depend on each other and Áine saw in Carole someone with the same drive and dedication which she brought to her own work.

At first Carole would operate as group leader, organising on the Irish side and shepherding her group until they arrived at Split or Dubrovnik Airport.

They would share the work of guiding people in the mountains. In the peak of summer the ascent would be made in the dark at 4am to avail of the coolest conditions, thus avoiding the experiences of those who got badly burned in the heat of the day.

But despite the fact that they spent so much time together, there was little enough time for personal exchanges.

More often than not over a pizza or a glass of wine they would discuss the needs of their pilgrims and make plans for the following days activity.

Carole would arrange special attention for those who were ill or with special needs, devise a rota for those who would mind them and they were always conscious of trying to provide the best of attention for those for whom they were responsible.

Through their work, a special bond was forged which would keep the women not only working together but dedicated to the same humanitarian cause even though they were a thousand miles apart.

The special relationship helped to bridge the gap between Áine's frequent requests for aid and Carole's appeals at home.

So, when war broke out and Aine phoned for Carole's help, it was inconceivable that Carole would refuse. She threw herself into her work on behalf of the refugees as eagerly and with as much commitment as she had done in Medjugorje.

No sooner would a list arrive by phone or fax, than Carole would start on its collection and the full extent of what she achieved for the people of Bosnia may never by fully realised.

5

THE HORRORS OF WAR

If there has been another country in the Western world which has suffered as much in war since 1945 as Bosnia/Hercegovina has done, then the collective media and governments have kept very quiet about it.

Whether it was a pre-planned campaign of butchery, torture and terror or whether it just fed off its own momentum once it got started, we may have to wait for some time to find out, but the savagery inflicted on the people of Bosnia/Hercegovina has been at times almost indescribable.

The dream of Slobodan Milosevic of creating a greater Serbia started long before he became President of Serbia in 1986, but it is clear that he was prepared to sacrifice a great deal in his desire to expand not only its borders but the economic and political power of Serbia as well.

He set about his task in a cold and clinical fashion. He employed every device and strategy to divide and conquer his opponents from deceit and lies to treachery and threats. With the complicity of the west through inaction and their ignoring of every lesson learned in the Second World War, Vietnam and Cambodia, Milosevic aided by his Bosnian chief ally Radovan Karadzic extracted a huge price from the people of Bosnia/Hercegovina for their audacity in opposing his blatant expansionism.

In the war zones of the former Yugoslavia, Slovenia, the first target of Serbian wrath had their army to defend them and because they had little to offer the Serbs strategically they were left largely alone.

Even Croatia, the second Republic to declare independence and merit the tyrannical attentions of Serbia, had formed their own army and had some measure of resources to counter the Serbian threat to their people in their homeland of neighbouring Bosnia.

A measure of the abandonment of the Bosnian Muslims and Croats by the combined Western powers was the failure of the U.N. to implement any effective policy of protection of the population.

Even in December 1992 when the General Assembly of the United Nations voted to exclude Bosnia/Hercegovina from the arms embargo on the former Republic of Yugoslavia, the Security council refused to ratify the decision. So Bosnian hands continued to be tied as their Serbian opponents landed blow after blow while the U.N. referee either watched with total disinterest or turned its collective back.

Even when the U.N. eventually put in troops to protect humanitarian aid convoys, they were shamefully used as a reason not to send in air-strikes against the Serbian artillery which daily pounded Sarajevo and other defenceless cities, lest they be the target for reprisals.

The Croats and Muslims could not be blamed for wondering whether or not it would have been better if the U.N. troops had been pulled out and the air-strikes sent in, such was their limited role in their protection.

Peace negotiator Lord Carrington acknowledged defeat in August 1992 and got out. After the failure of the Vance/Owen Peace Plan in May 1993, Cyrus Vance left too.

All that was left of the E.C./U.N. negotiating team was Britain's Lord Owen who might as easily have conceded defeat at that stage as continue talks in Geneva through the Summer of 1993 which were little more than a sham.

Always the Muslims and Croats were the losers. They had been invaded by the Serbs and had their lands annexed. Their people suffered horribly in a wanton campaign of genocide by Serbian Forces and there seemed to be no friend on whom they could rely for help.

As they resisted attempts to have a disgraceful settlement imposed on them at the peace negotiations they were represented as the ones dragging their heels. The oppressed were seen as anti-peace, the ones holding up the settlement of the conflict even as they watched their allocated territory reduce almost weekly.

Against this background of inaction sometimes seeming to border on blatant discrimination by the West, it was hardly surprising that the old woman told Carole Wiley high on a mountain at Ulog that even Heaven seemed to have forgotten them.

Never since the Jews had been transported across Europe in cattle wagons or the Cambodians had been forced to relocate by Pol Pot had a civilian population suffered so much. Never had they been used in such a cynical fashion as military pawns as they fell victims of the revived practice of ethnic cleansing.

The term ethnic cleansing could almost have been coined by the same person who described lying as being economical with the truth or saying terminate with extreme prejudice when they really meant murder.

But ethnic cleansing is older than those other phrases and disguises an act, at once vicious, premeditated and full of hatred. If old enmities were revived then they had good reason to be. The hatred of generations was really only a myth but in a short few months the seeds were sown for generations of hatred to come.

And how plentiful those seeds had been sown, how quickly the sowers were on hand after the declaration of independence. It is difficult to imagine how so many candidates could emerge so quickly to carry out the murders and massacres, the butchery and torture, the depraved and satanic acts of barbarism for which this war has become tragically known.

Where else in a society claiming to be modern, could men wrench children from the arms of their distraught mothers and fling them before their horror-stricken parents into a furnace.

Where else would children be snatched from a pavement and have their arms and legs cut off to be left to die. Their only crime being that they were of Muslim or Croatian stock. Where else would a child have its throat cut in the street just because of what he or she represents.

A refugee told Carole of one of the earlier massacres of this war involving the shelling of a kindergarten school where all fifty-nine children and their teachers were killed. Later the Serb soldiers responsible came and took the bodies from the wreckage and carefully laid them out in lines in the street. Then before a watching video camera, they systematically slit the throat of each of the dead children and teachers. It was, she was told later shown on local television with the warning that that was what anyone could expect who did not conform.

Slitting of throats has been brought to a fine art in this war, a skill which is practised on pigs until it has been perfected.

One of the least documented, though most mentioned horrors of this war has been that of the rape camps. Women were always deemed the legitimate spoils of war. Like every other atrocity in this conflict, this too has been taken to the ultimate with the provision of what have become known as rape-camps for the benefit of soldiers returning from the front line.

Here groups of women and girls from the most junior to grandmothers are kept in detention for long periods and made available to the soldiers as they arrive from the front. Naturally no thought is given to the women who are used and abused until exhaustion or death claims them.

There is on record the testimony of one twelve-year old girl who through the course of one day was raped twenty-seven times. Who can even guess at the psychological damage, the physical injury which had been inflicted on her as she suffered her long hours of private and public torture.

Is there any more heinous act which can be perpetrated on a woman than rape. What then can this shell of a person be like after being subjected to such barbarism not once or twice in a day, but twenty-seven times.

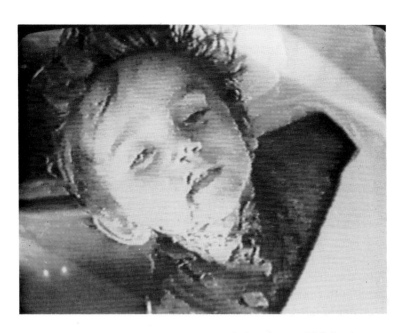

A child with his throat cut, one more victim of war which has been particularly brutal on children.

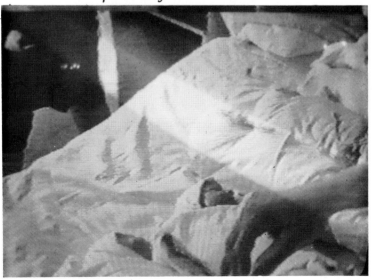

*Slaughter of the innocents . . .
A line of little bodies, proof of the inhumanity of the war.*

The following, with names deleted, from the Amnesty International advertisement of July 1992 did not refer to Bosnia, but it might well have:-

"She ran all the way to the spot and found her husband's body still nailed to the tree. In a rage of horror and grief - hardly knowing what she was doing, she started back for help. She had almost reached home when an evil chance brought her face to face with the soldiers who had killed her husband. They showed their pity for the sobbing woman by gang-raping her. A week later the same soldiers took her and her twelve-year old sister to the Army camp, where they were locked in a room with about forty other female captives. Soldiers would enter the room, choose a woman and repeatedly rape her in front of all the others. She said "after five days my sister's little heart could take it no more. She went into convulsions and died. When the soldiers saw that I, too, could take no more, they freed me"

Was that the way it was for the women of Bosnia/ Hercegovina who had already lost husbands and homes and now, according to their religion and law, their honour too?

For Muslim women, rape has an even greater significance. Thereafter they will be shunned by their families and when and if a baby is born then it too will be abandoned by its mother. The family will leave the area never to return, thus assisting in the process of ethnic cleansing.

In Ireland, indeed in most developed countries, there is usually someone to listen, someone to give help or advice and to give support through the trauma just experienced. A Muslim woman cannot even disclose her ordeal for fear of being shunned, cut off from her family and left to fend for herself.

Many Muslim women go into hospitals, have their babies and walk out leaving them behind. It is a part of their lives which is too difficult to deal with.

There is another reported story of a young Italian priest who was on a humanitarian mission to a maternity hospital in a town in Croatia where there were nineteen women waiting to have their babies. The soldiers came and took the women out to the back of the hospital where they slit their stomachs, removed their babies and stamped them underfoot.

There were few survivors and the priest, who was made to witness those barbarous acts is now in a mental hospital in Italy. Many of the atrocities involve pregnant women and foetuses and one of the most loathsome cases which doctors have had to regularly deal with is the man's body which is brought to them with the stomach slashed and stapled together again.

They know that when they investigate the wound they will find a human foetus inside. Sometimes the trousers will just have been pulled up over the incision and tied off with a belt or string. The woman from whom the foetus was taken will have had her stomach filled with sand and the large cut stapled closed. Any normal medical condition they have been trained and prepared for, but this barbarism they will never get used to. Who can do this to his fellow man or woman. A soldier, or is it Satan-inspired? Carole takes consolation in her belief that normal soldiers would not indulge in these practices. She has learned that they are given drugs before being sent out to do these dirty deeds or are high on rakije, the local liquor.

The soldiers are equally inventive when it comes to torturing men. Invariably, the process starts with the removal of finger- and toenails with a pliers, cigarettes are stubbed out on the body and then the gasoline treatment is commenced.

This involves inflicting hundreds of small cuts all over the body with a razor blade. The victims are then immersed in petrol and have little difficulty in screaming with agony. While the screaming lasts, they are left alive but if they stop they are shot. People learn quickly to keep shouting and screaming and hoarse though they might be they still manage to find a sound. To stop is to die.

In one documented instance it went on for hours and few survived. Those who did were taken out and made to dig their own graves. As the size of the graves got larger they were made to step in and out, in and out, continually. At some point a soldier would approach a prisoner, tell him to stay in and shoot him at point blank range.

Finally, three of the number were able to stay mobile, and were taken back in a half dead condition to their shed accommodation. One of the soldiers that day who recognised the excesses to which he was a party tried as diplomatically as he could to get the soldiers to stop, but he had little success.

He later discovered a group of local men approaching the camp attempting to effect a rescue. He refrained from sounding the alarm and the remaining prisoners were rescued. He defected a short time later. His testimony tells of the torture and murder by the Cetnik irregulars who support the Serbian cause.

Capture for a Croatian or Muslim soldier by the Cetniks means guaranteed torture and death. Croatian soldiers usually carry a rosary beads around their necks which they are immediately made to swallow. Many of them choke or smother in the process. If they do not have a rosary then their genitals are cut off and they are made to swallow those. Doctors have often found such remains in the stomachs of soldiers.

There is one Cetnik woman who specialises in a particularly obnoxious torture. With a sharpened spoon she will gouge out the eyes of the soldier and spoon the resultant mess into their mouths which they are then made to swallow. The ears are torn off and they might have limbs chopped off as well. Being a woman is no guarantee of safety in this war as the tens of thousands who have passed through the rape camps have found out. They too have been subjected to the "conventional" tortures before being made to kneel in front of their graves and be decapitated.

In addition to those tortures which were carried out with no apparent objective, captured soldiers were used in whatever way they could. They were placed strategically as a human shield against the possibility of a ground assault by the United Nations or NATO troops, though the Serbs need not have worried, invasion was never apparently on the agenda of either body.

There were reports too that they were used as a live blood supply for the Serb dominated Federal Army, and it is said that many were drained of almost their entire blood supply to facilitate the Serb war machine.

There was no room for dissent in the Serb military code and those who did were given little scope for what would be perceived as treason. There was one reported case of several Serb soldiers being hanged by their own officers on a bridge and their bodies being left for days as a warning to others "to conform".

One of the first recorded massacres of the war in Croatia was during the attack on Vukovar in August 1991. It is estimated that up to seven thousand people were killed during a nine-hour orgy of murder and the returning survivors were met by appalling sights. Heads had been cut off and acid had been thrown on people's bodies. Even in death, their faces were contorted with pain and for them eventual death came as a merciful release.

Bits of bodies littered the streets among those who had been shot or stabbed or died from the shelling. Obviously some men had been tied to several vehicles which were driven away in opposite directions giving the effect of the rack of old. This was not done quickly, torture never is. The vehicles were inched apart, stretching the limbs of the unfortunate between. At the last minute and to prolong the stretch and agony as long as possible the stomach is slashed open to spill the intestines along the ground. Finally the body comes apart, hopefully killing the victim quickly in the process. The grisly remains are a testimony on the video to the grave inhumanity which man can still inflict on his fellow men.

The footage of the mass grave being opened, the quick-lime assisted decaying bodies are not a pretty sight, but massacres and other violations of human rights must be documented for future use. War crimes, no matter by whom committed must be paid for and reports of atrocities by Muslims and Croats must in time be investigated fully too. Vengeance may have driven

A charred body, one more victim in a war which has claimed hundreds of thousands of lives.

From a mass grave . Quicklime was often used to hasten decomposition to prevent identification of remains. The victim's watch still clings to the decomposing wrist.

them to excesses against other ethnic groups and it is regrettable that in a war which was started and sustained by the Serbs, which has caused such personal misery and the carve-up of Bosnia/Hercegovina, should now have created war criminals among the people who under other circumstances would be farmers, businessmen and factory workers. There are few winners in war. The battlefields, streets and wrecked homes are littered with losers.

In remote regions of Bosnia personal feuds and vendettas are played out daily. Local differences between Muslim, Croat and Serb are brought to solution and there is no doubt that as in any war, excesses have been committed by all sides. Temporary local alliances are forged between the most unlikely partners, to accommodate local conditions which often do not reflect the position nationally.

This in another tragedy of the war. The atrocities feed on themselves and soon all sides have incidents to answer for. But those who started it all, those who continue the war, those who have inflicted most of the savagery, those who have cynically targeted individuals, communities, villages, towns and cities are the Serbs and if international justice is not to be a farce, then they must be held accountable up to the highest levels in time.

In an early appeal in Cork of which Carole and Áine were a part, it was reported that in April 1992 an estimated two thousand people were massacred in the town of Bijelina near the Serbian border in Bosnia. Their bodies were bulldozed into a mass grave. While this was happening, the Serbian Army refused entry to the town to the United Nations troops and EC Monitors but they were later present to witness the opening of the mass grave when the relations came to dig up their dead.

In the neighbouring town of Foca nobody knows how many were massacred but it is known that there are over three hundred orphaned children in one small clinic and a consignment of aid that was destined for this clinic was confiscated by the Serbian Army.

But not all the horrors of this war were major massacres. Press reports over the last two years tell their own story. A twenty-one year old Muslim girl from a village near Kozarac was reported in August 1992 to have been forced, with a knife at her throat, to burn down her family's home and then set fire to another nine houses. Her captors threatened to slit her throat and cut out her eyes before she was finally taken to the internment camp at Trnopolje. On the way she saw bodies littering the roadside in other Muslim communities.

Another woman of fifty-four said she saw a Serbian guard shoot a woman dead while she breast-fed her baby. He apparently had been angered by her other child wandering out of the room alone. She said rape was commonplace. Masked drunken men would come in and take the people's teenage daughters. They would tell them the girls would be back in a couple of hours. "Then you would just hear the screams". (Irish Independent 7/8/92).

Daniel McGregory writing for the Irish Independent from Sarajevo describes in some detail the horror of living in a city under siege, and it was but five months old at that stage

"There wasn't a flicker of light in this shelter, the fifty or so children here could not see their mothers, only cling to them for comfort. Erika Madchik's baby Elma has known no other existence. "She was born the day after the war started so she has never seen the sun nor felt its warmth on her face. She has never touched or smelt a flower. What way is this to live?"

Then there was the case of little Kemal Karic who at four months had the distinction of being the youngest patient in the Sarajevo Hospital to have lost a limb.

"His mother could stand no more of a recent night's bombardment so (she) ran from her apartment to a shelter. A mortar exploded in their path killing her and wounding Kemal. He lay beside his mother's corpse until the firing subsided enough for a neighbour to rescue him"

In the graveyards, often makeshift ones in parks and boulevards, mourners cannot spend long burying their dead or they too will become targets. Often funerals have to be abandoned for several hours to await a lull in the shelling, and graves can be quite shallow with workers unable to get enough time to go the required depth.

It is this cynical targeting not just of the civilian population but people in essential services such as doctors and paramedics, water, electricity and telephone workers and of course the readily identifiable Red Cross which makes many of the actions in this war both cowardly and dastardly.

Even those who stop to chat in front of the U.N. building in Sarajevo are not safe. A mortar fell among a group there, killing them and up to sixteen others who were in the street at the time.

There is particularly grisly footage of the aftermath of a mortar attack on a queue at a bakery. As the smoke clears there are dead, dying and injured all around, copious quantities of blood spilled over the pavements. Victims lie on the ground in shock or prop themselves against buildings and watch their life-blood drain away in a red rivulet towards the gutter. The screams of the survivors are pitiful to hear but there will be no welcoming wail of sirens as ambulances rush to the injured. There are few services left.

It is what Enniskillen must have been like, without the rubble, the Greysteel, Darkley and others with which we have become familiar. Thankfully, in this country, atrocities of that magnitude are few. In Sarajevo, Mostar and the other besieged towns of Bosnia/Hercegovina, it is a daily occurrence and there are few left to sweep up the human debris in the aftermath.

The religious, a section of society who traditionally remained untouched by war, have been drawn into the conflict in Bosnia/Hercegovina like any other. Many have fallen victim to the fighting but that is not where it has ended. In the early summer of 1993, three priests and three nuns were captured and tortured for a long time in Konjic. Despite attempts by the U.N. it was not possible to effect their release.

On 16th June 1992 in the Novo Topolo convent near Banja Luka it was reported that twenty nuns were captured and subjected to every kind of maltreatment including rape by Serbian militiamen. Who can imagine the horror and abuse that was heaped on these women who suffered as horribly as their Muslim sisters, or women from the Croatian community.

In every conflict in Europe in the last century, churches and shrines have been regarded as sacred and have been granted immunity. Rome itself in the last war was declared an open city, but in the war in the Balkans, it has been open season on church and mosque as well as the people who serve and worship there.

In every town that has been attacked by the Serbs, churches and mosques have been destroyed. Even in Banja Luka, where there has been little fighting in the town, all fifteen mosques and many of the churches have been destroyed. While the soldiers themselves may not be Communist, many of those who control them certainly are and it appears as if the former Yugoslavia will take a considerable time to rid itself of the ideology which held it and much of Eastern Europe back for the last three quarters of a century.

But the most heart-rending stories of all to emerge from a land of horror have been those of the starvation of the people. As Irish people with an understanding of our own history, we can readily identify with the stories of starvation which have emanated from many parts of Bosnia/Hercegovina.

Carole, Áine, Fr. Sean O'Driscoll and Eamonn Timmins from the Cork Examiner heard first hand the stories from the women of Ulog of going out to pick grass to boil, to put something, anything, in the stomachs of their children. In Sarajevo, the people regularly made soup of grass and dandelions, something which no doubt happened in the many besieged cities and towns there.

The term hungry grass in Ireland has a particular meaning. During the Great Hunger of 1847-49 with the grain being exported and the failure of the potato crop in successive years,

Grisly remains, a tray of testicles discovered after a massacre.

A typical sight in Bosnia., a queue forms in the hope of getting some bread. Later such queues were to become a target for mortar attack.

people collapsed on the roadsides from weakness induced by hunger.

As they lay dying, their instinct for survival drove them to chew on the grass on which they lay. For many it was their last act before death finally took them from their misery. But conditions in Bosnia/Hercegovina are always worse and in February 1993 there came reports from Eastern Bosnia that the people there were skinning and eating their dead to survive.

This horrified the world, though the governments were quick to settle back into their torpor after their usual ineffective gesture. It did however galvanise U.N. Commander, General Philippe Morillon into action and in a memorable encounter first faced down the Serbs to enter Srebrenica, one of the worst off of the towns of Eastern Bosnia , and then further defied them by staying until the arrival of a food convoy.

It was a good victory though Srebrenica fell shortly after, but the name of Morillon will be remembered with pride in Eastern Bosnia for a very long time to come. The west did carry out some air-drops of food and medical supplies but they were few, clumsy, inaccurate and largely ineffective.

The horrors of war are not just the massacres large and small, the murder, torture and rape. They are also to be found in the curtailment of everyday living, the deprivation of everyday services, the suspension of everyday rights, all of the things we take for granted.

For the widow, it is the loss of her husband, killed, missing or captured and she is left to carry the burden of caring for her children alone in a very hostile environment.

It is the pain of the old man who has spent fifty days in a concentration camp and cannot talk about his experiences there.

It is in the pain of the child who suffers the trauma of an operation to cure a war injury without the benefit of an anaesthetic. It is the pain of the doctor who has to carry out that operation for which no training can be adequate.

It is the pain of the people who knew better times, had good living standards, good homes and enough to eat. For most of them that is now gone. They have been forced to become refugees, hunted from home and village while their property is stolen by the state.

These are the rights which we take for granted every day, rights we do not have to think about or campaign for. For the people of Bosnia it is a different matter and as they go into their third year of war, they know that things cannot get much worse for them. For most the light of hope has flickered out and few now look to the west for salvation. They no longer expect to hear the bugle call or see the blue of the cavalry ride over the hill. They are on their own and they know it.

6

GOING PUBLIC

Invariably, a phone call starts Carole's working day. After Tony is gone to work and the children are delivered to school the everyday housewife may think of a steadying cup of coffee and a quiet cigarette if she smokes.

There may even be time to drop in to a friends house to share thoughts, opinions, fears, good news or bad, across the kitchen table or ironing board. This is a luxury Carole can afford only rarely. Jan, Carole's near neighbour and close friend, is always there and available, a few steps or a phone call away, sometimes no more than a wish distant and Carole is grateful for the security which her friend represents in her life.

For Carole Wiley, the phone has become an inseparable part of her life and sometimes Tony wonders if surgery will be required to part it from her hand and ear.

It was a phonecall which triggered a major change in the Wiley household and which saw Carole add to her everyday household chores the additional demanding role of aid worker.

Few can realise what that simple phrase means but for Carole it represents, hours of telephone time arranging food and medicine, talking with the ad hoc groups who feed their supplies into the warehouse, and money into the Bank Account and making arrangements for fund-raising events.

In November 1992 during one of her regular calls Aine said that the hospital was desperately in need of X-ray film. They had run out some time before and without this vital medical aid, the doctors were only guessing at putting people back together.

There were many patients with spinal injuries and doctors were afraid they would end up paralysed as a result of treatment "in the dark".

Carole managed to get a consignment together, but because independent transport was no longer operating properly in the country she decided to fly out with the precious film herself.

She was shocked by what she saw there. Things had changed immeasurably since last she had been there about a year previously with a group of pilgrims and she now better understood Áine's pleas.

The sight of the broken down building, the make-shift beds, the use of corridors for wards because the rooms were destroyed, took her aback. Operations were being carried out in pathology baths and the walls were blackened in places from the use of candles.

In the windows, used x ray film kept out the wind but kept little heat in and it darkened the rooms considerably. Shocked though she was, the visit did have its humorous moments. As they walked along the makeshift men's corridor/ward Áine turned to Carole and said "Take care passing here".

Carole did not understand what she meant, at least not in time for as she passed a particular bed a hand snaked out to clutch her leg and a crafty cackle told her she had fallen foul of the hospital lecher. It was the first laughter in the hospital for a long time and raised the men's spirits.

The patients were high in morale but low in even the most basic luxuries. Most craved a cigarette but could not afford it though by our standards they would be a cheap commodity in the shops, due to the widespread growing of tobacco. The need for a cigarette was clear in the patients eyes and Carole took action. She got a lift to the market and with the aid of the driver, using her personal emergency money supply, which she had brought to deal with any unforeseen circumstances, she purchased cartons of cigarettes.

Back in the hospital she distributed them among the patients and doctors who were thrilled with their unexpected windfall, but it gave Carole an early insight at first hand of the real hardships for the patients of Bosnia.

Transport of the goods to Bosnia was one of the most worrying and most expensive parts of the operation.

At first they would get a loan of a lorry and ferry the aid directly to Mostar but as conditions steadily deteriorated there, they found it more difficult to convince lorry owners that they had nothing to fear.

On a previous occasion when they employed such a method they had the lorry loaded and ready to go to the boat after the driver had got a few hours sleep. There was a particularly bad news bulletin that night and the owner arrived at the warehouse looking for his lorry back. Everything was ready and Carole did not want to delay the consignment any further. She argued with him for a long time but nothing would move him. His mind was made up.

Finally, he agreed to allow the lorry to go if Carole signed a personal guarantee for £18,000 that he would be re-imbursed for any damage to his lorry over the two weeks it would be gone.

On her usual impulse, Carole signed and placed her fate, once more in the hands of the Blessed Virgin. She couldn't bring herself to tell Tony what she had done and she had a few nervous days while the lorry was in the war zone, but she relied on her prayers and the purpose of the enterprise for the Blessed Virgin to look after the driver, lorry and cargo.

It turned out to be the least troublesome journey they had ever had, with no weather difficulties, mechanical failure or bureaucratic delays. But Carole had learned her lesson and realised just how much of a chance she had taken, particularly without consulting Tony.

Carole would occasionally go to Mostar to help distribute the supplies and bring special emergency drugs or equipment with her.

On one such trip, the women had a long and serious look at the operation and felt that changes were needed. Carole and Aine decided to go it alone and launched their own appeal. While Áine looked after the Bosnia side, Carole would organise the necessary supplies in Ireland.

Suitable arrangements were made with the financial institutions with which they dealt in regard to their funds. Carole's brother Gerard was an invaluable help in this, drawing on his experience in the financial world to help her set up proper structures. He and his wife Carmel have continued to be a source of strength and encouragement when the going gets tough and the paperwork difficult, and are people on whom Carole relies a great deal.

All of Carole's energies which she dedicated to their enterprise were used to the full. Likewise her co-workers were more concerned with getting the job done than merely deciding to do it, and they felt no loss at not having to attend meetings. They worked when they had the time and made the extra effort when a container had to be got ready.

Carole was out of the house much less and consulted with her fellow workers by phone. Her father, through his contacts in Fords had secured the use of a warehouse in their old factory which had been transformed into The Marina Commercial Park. Originally the agreement had been for a week but they have been there since.

It seemed to be the ideal arrangement and as the last two years has proved, it was.

Áine arrived in Ireland before Christmas 1992 to a joyous homecoming and now the two women could make plans for further publicising their work, extending the area of their appeal and getting more containers out to Bosnia.

Aine had little to tell Carole that was new on the war. She had given her all the horrific reports on Carole's various visits with aid and Carole had become progressively numbed as she listened to reports of an ever-worsening situation.

The two women, very conscious that they were two lone women, trying to alleviate suffering in a war which had targeted women, sat down to plan their campaign.

They relied on a small number of volunteers who helped when and where they were required without the need for a title or formal recognition.

They set about contacting suppliers, hospitals and stores for the necessary items and others canvassed businesses or held collections to raise funds to buy the goods.

They met with varying degrees of success but by March they had a container full and it was despatched to Áine who by this time had returned to Bosnia and who arranged for its distribution around the hospitals.

Dr. Martinovic, the Chief Surgeon in Mostar Hospital was ecstatic with the response and a second container arrived in April and with growing frequency thereafter.

Áine kept in regular contact with Carole telling her what was needed and acting as a conduit between Carole and Dr. Martinovic.

But primarily Carole was concerned to let the world know what was happening on Europe's doorstep. She could not understand how so many reporters could have been covering the war, how so much video footage could have been taken out of the country, yet so many people in responsible places did not seem to know the full or true story.

Massacres had been taking place for over a year, the rape camps had been discovered and photos of the concentration camps had been published around the world, but still the governments did little or nothing.

She was bitterly disappointed by the worlds' response, totally disenchanted with the lack of American commitment and disgusted that the E.C. had not galvanised support within their own ranks and elsewhere, for some kind of initiative, either political or military to stop the ravaging of a country she had grown to love.

When Aine was in Ireland, a newspaper friend had suggested that they get in contact with Aras an Uachtaráin to seek a meeting with President Robinson and he promised to use his contacts to smooth their path.

Carole had been in touch with the Kenny Live office and Katherine Cahill had expressed an interest in seeing the tapes of the atrocities which Áine had brought back with her with a view to including an item on the show. There was a problem with this however, and it is also one which Carole has consistently had to face. Most of the footage is too gruesome for general audiences, so it can not be shown on television lest children are watching. It is frustrating but it is one of the constraints of the medium.

After an interview on R.T.E.s News at One programme from Cork, Aine was contacted by the then Minister for Foreign Affairs Mr. David Andrews for a first hand account of the situation.

Carole had not neglected the political side either and continued to make approaches to his Department. David Andrews had taken a keen and active interest in the Yugoslav conflict and had been strong in his condemnation of the atrocities, particularly those against women and his commitment had seemed genuine.

Carole was hopeful that if they could meet with Minister Andrews and show him the tapes, that he was the kind of person to initiate action. However it had not been long since the General Election and the political situation in Ireland was fluid. It looked as if there would be a coalition between Fianna Fáil and Labour so Carole was hopeful that David Andrews would continue in Foreign Affairs.

She was hopeful too that since the United Nations had asked him to formally investigate the rape camp allegations he would enjoy greater support on the international scene.

So it was with great hope and confidence that the women set out that Friday morning on the train to Dublin. They expected a positive response from their high level meetings and determined they would make the best of their opportunities. They chatted alternately about life in Medjugorje and Mostar and their impending meetings and took advantage of the four hours they sat together in the railway carriage to bring each other up to date on their own lives.

They were met at Heuston Station by Carole's Uncle, Declan Bennett who would be their chauffeur and guide around the city for the next few days. They were delighted with this for not alone did it save them the frustration of chasing taxis and buses but it helped considerably with their budgets as well.

They were excited at the prospect of making progress at last and lost no time in heading for Aras an Uachtaráin. They were met by the Presidential Aide Bride Rosney who told them the format of the meeting and welcomed them to the Presidential Residence. Coffee and biscuits were served and she chatted about the house and its history.

Áine was photographed with the President and then they retired to an inner room with Bride Rosney. The Presidents Aide de Camp rejoined Carole and her uncle and over tea waited for the meeting to finish.

Carole savoured the feeling of richness around her and slipped off her shoes to feel the deep pile of the carpet. She loved the paintings, silverware and furniture, and was particularly impressed by the corridor outside the reception room which was lined with the busts of previous incumbents.

She wondered how Áine was getting on inside and said a mental prayer that their mission would be successful. She had no doubt that the Galway girl would acquit herself well and not be overawed by the occasion.

When she emerged Áine was smiling so Carole knew it had gone well, "you got to see the house" Áine whispered, as they left the reception room. "You got to meet the President" Carole countered, and the two laughed as they went down the steps.

Áine would love to have taken the grand tour but their schedule was tight and they had to prepare for their R.T.E. appearance later.

As Uncle Declan drove them away Áine gave Carole a brief outline of what had transpired. Carole and Áine had been very impressed with the reception they had got and felt the meeting had been successful.

Uncle Declan took them home to eat, and they found that his wife Joan had prepared a huge lunch for them. It had been a long morning and they did their meal justice. With a long evening and night to come they were not sure when they would get to eat again.

They had to recount their story to their hostess who was pleased that they had got on so well.

That afternoon they spent preparing for their trip to R.T.E. and were like two schoolgirls getting ready for a party. There was hair to be washed and arranged which naturally fell to Carole, clothes to be pressed and make-up applied.

The women were in high good humour and managed to complete their preparations in time. Just as they were finishing late in the afternoon the phone rang.

R.T.E. were on to say that a car would be there for them soon and please do not wear white, polka dots or stripes. Luckily the girls had not selected the prohibited colour schemes but wondered what they would have done that late, on a Saturday evening if they'd had.

Here they were in Dublin and all their clothes were a hundred and fifty miles away in Cork. Áine had opted for a green round necked edge to edge jacket with a black skirt while Carole wore a black two piece.

Sometime later a knock came to the door and the R.T.E. car was announced. As she came face to face with the driver, he smiled and said "Well Carole Owens, is this what you're doing now". Myles Cullen was an old friend and close neighbour from their Dublin days who now worked for the national television station and spent his day ferrying celebrities around.

As they drove to Montrose they spoke of old times, exchanged memories and brought each other up-to-date on their families. Carole was nervous even though she would have little to do on the programme but her meeting with Myles settled her down considerably.

There were three seats within camera range, reserved for Carole, Uncle Declan and a friend of Aine's, John Gaffney, and after a drink in the hospitality suite they took their places.

Aine made very good use of her twenty minutes or so, telling the country what precisely was happening. There were two segments of her tape run during the interview but they were not really representative of the horrors the population was experiencing.

In her seat Carole felt a quiet satisfaction that they were now achieving part of their objective which was raising the public consciousness about the situation in Bosnia. Public pressure would result from this exposure and Carole's main task, the gathering of aid in Ireland, would probably be a little easier and more successful. She also hoped that it might inspire people to pray a little more fervently and a little more often, for an end to this satanic war.

As well, Pat Kenny would understand the situation better, having met Carole and Áine, and he might be in a position on a later programme on radio or television to influence public opinion.

After the show they spoke to Pat for a long time and he promised to stay in touch and do what he could for them in the future.

Appearing on the programme that night also was Niamh Kavanagh who was singing her entry for the Eurovision Song Contest. Having heard it Carole was convinced it would win and told Niamh so, saying she had never been wrong in the years she had made a Eurovision prediction.

The following Spring as Niamh sang her way to success in front of a billion people, Carole felt like ringing her up and saying "Did I not tell you".

It was almost two in the morning before they were home. Aunt Joan was impressed by Áine's contribution and told her so. The women briefly reviewed the day before turning in and concluded that their two days in the capital had been well spent.

It was over now to those to whom they had spoken, the President, the government representatives and the people.

For Carole it was back to the campaign for food, medicine and funds for when the lorries could roll again. There was much to be planned, discussed and organised if their new independent joint approach was to succeed. They had discussions with solicitors and bankers and were eager to do things properly and fulfil all the conditions to become a recognised charity.

It was only mid January and yet something concrete had been achieved already. She wondered what this New Year would bring and what it would be like in 1993. Surely the world could not continue to stand by, she thought, and at Mass on Sunday morning with Tony and the children she prayed for an end to conflict everywhere. She wondered to herself if anything would ever melt the hearts of stone which ordered and carried out the atrocities in Bosnia, Northern Ireland, the Sudan and the many other trouble spots of the world. As she knelt in the church she recalled hearing that there were fifty four conflicts raging even as she prayed. There seemed to be no limits to mans' ingenuity for evil expressed so eloquently in the war in the Balkans.

In the comfort of their home she was haunted by the memory of what she had seen on her last trip and of what was contained in her tapes.

Her New Years resolution was for more prayer and more aid for the people she had come to know so well in the last six years. She was hopeful that the new aid line would short-circuit the red tape and would become an effective force in alleviating the suffering in Bosnia.

Quick decisions, and quick action brought quick results. It would be a long road in the new year to set up the contacts she needed, but with Tony, her parents and family behind her she could do it. She would certainly make it her priority.

7

WEDNESDAY 6TH OCTOBER

The campaign has been hectic, the material is flooding into the warehouse but the long hours of sorting, packing, labelling and taping the boxes have taken their toll.

She had been at the warehouse until late the night before and the warm feeling of her bed is inviting this morning. However the chores of the everyday housewife must be done and first and foremost there is breakfast and school.

The needs, demands and tensions of any four children home are many and varied and the Wiley children are no different to others. Time seems to slip by faster in the mornings as the 8.30 deadline for leaving approaches.

The day has yet to be planned and organised, but while Tony and the children devour and digest a variety of cereals, tea, toast and marmalade, Carole takes the opportunity to make the beds and spruce up the rooms.

She thinks to herself that someday the children may get around to doing these things for themselves. She feels exhausted but determined to maintain normality and ushers the now ready children to the car to be ferried to their various schools.

As she says good-bye to Audrey, who is last on the delivery route she feels able to relax for the first time. With a slightly sinking feeling she realises that there is a big Country and Western bash for Bosnia on in Dungarvan that night.

Once more the waves of exhaustion wash over her and she resolves to tell the Dungarvan people that she couldn't possibly go. She doesn't really want to bring Tony out that night and mind made up she turns for home and whatever news the dozen or so calls she expects will bring.

She resumes her housework and will have her chores including ironing completed by 10.30 a.m. Fr. Pat Butler who has done an enormous amount of work on the "Go Country for Bosnia" night, rings in to check that Carole will be along at the Park Hotel that night.

He explains that seven major artists and bands from the cream of the Irish Country and Western scene have agreed to appear free of charge and if at all possible she should attend.

It is sixty miles to Dungarvan which is not too bad but another sixty home in the wee small hours of the morning is not at all inviting. It's an imposition on Tony, a further drain on personal finances for petrol and a baby-sitter and they both could do with an early night.

She promises to review the situation in the afternoon but is careful to suggest that she will more than likely not travel.

Jan, her near neighbour and best friend drops in for coffee and Carole tells her that they will not travel. The thought of a long soak in a hot bath, something which has become more and more of a luxury in recent times, is attractive and followed by a long night's sleep is a delicious prospect.

Jan agrees that she is wise not to go. She tells Carole that she even looks overtired and that the campaign is taking its toll. They leave it at that and over a light lunch discuss family matters, girl talk and put the cares of the day behind them.

With a meeting with the Lord Mayor and Lady Mayoress coming up at 5.00 and two containers coming into the warehouse from Galway and Cashel there will be little time for preparing dinner later, so before she leaves to pick up Kristian at 2.30 she prepares a solid evening meal and is about to leave for the school when the phone rings.

It is one of the Dungarvan Group and he wants to know if she will come after all. She is still reluctant but the voice is persuasive and he points out that all the indications are that it will be big, enjoyable and financially successful, and that she and the committee owe it to the bands to be there. A guarantee of 11 o'clock departure is an added offer and she falters.

Some of the recent fund-raising events had yielded little and she agrees that a successful night would be a tonic.

Recklessly, she says she'll go. She has good friends there and County Waterford was one of the first areas to start sending her aid for Bosnia.

Now it is a race against time. She picks up Kristian, Audrey and Mark and arrives at the warehouse in time to see one of the containers arriving. Some of her small army of loyal workers including her father have turned up to help and by four o'clock as she leaves, most of the mountain of material has been safely brought inside.

A quick dash back to Carrigaline to collect Sarah and start the dinner. A quick change of clothes brings her almost to the deadline and despite her best efforts it will be at least five-thirty before she reaches City Hall..

She says good-bye to the children and sits into the car knowing it will be another nine or ten hours and a hundred and fifty miles before she can relax in bed. A daunting prospect.

The Lady Mayoress has invited Carole to her reception to see the format of the Fashion Show in which she is involved on behalf of St. Patrick's Hospital.

A glance around the room shows her that many of the City's influential women are there together with representatives of the model agency and the stores taking part.

After the formalities, the Lady Mayoress is eager to hear about Carole's' work in Ireland and Áine's role in Bosnia, and she has a willing narrator in Carole who avails of the opportunity to bring the City's First Lady up to date.

So engrossed are they in their discussion, breaking occasionally only for the Lady Mayoress to say good-bye to her guests, that by the time they finish they discover the room is empty. But the evening has been successful for both of them. The reception was well attended and received, and Carole had found a new ally.

They had discussed Bosnia and their families, children and the problem of coping under pressure, life in the public eye and the value of privacy, something which Carole surrendered three years ago.

She leaves City Hall for Eglington Street to meet with Tony for the drive to Dungarvan.

It is a fine evening and the trip is pleasant, with Youghal Bay looking particularly attractive as they drive down the Prom.

Carole tells Tony of her day, brings him up to date on the children and recounts the happenings at City Hall. He too is pleased with her evening and delighted to hear that the Lady Mayoress had offered to be Patron of the Áine and Carole Fund.

Tony hopes that the Dungarvan people will have something ready to eat. He's starving and they debate about stopping at a restaurant.

Luckily they don't for when they arrive weary and hungry they are met by a bright-eyed and enthusiastic committee who have laid on a sumptuous spread for the Bands and guests.

As they tuck in with a will, they are told that ticket sales are good and that people will begin arriving shortly and also there should be a huge response on the night.

The first of the bands and artists arrive. Paddy O'Brien and his musicians, local man Richie Halpin and a vivacious Trudi Lawlor in her usual good humour. The artists trade compliments, best wishes and a few in-jokes from the business.

They are introduced all round, fed and despatched to the stage to prepare for the 9 o'clock start. Fr. Pat Butler who has put the entertainment package together presides over the stage arrangements and the men at the door are already busy with an early stream of fans.

This is a unique event and there is no doubt it will be a sell-out. One by one the artists are introduced to Carole and she finds it is the tonic she needed. Thoughts of the sixty mile drive home are shelved for the moment. She becomes immersed in the happy atmosphere, confident that the success of the evening will go a long way towards paying the cost of the transport of a container.

Some of the Committee of the West Waterford Bosnia Awarness Group at their successful "Go Country for Bosnia" night in the Park Hotel, Dungarvan.

"Go Country for Bosnia" one more successful show and in the small hours of the morning, Carole accepts a substantial cheque and a bouquet of flowers from organiser Fr. Pat Butler in the Rhu Glenn, Co. Kilkenny.

She is whisked away from talking with Declan Nerney, Pat Hayes and Jimmy Buckley to give her now customary talk to the audience.

She is hesitant at first, a little nervous despite the number of times she has spoken on the subject before but after a minute or two she is well on her way.

She speaks of atrocities, of severed limbs, wounded women, children operated on without anaesthetics. Her listeners grimace and shiver as she details each painful scene she has seen in the Hospitals of Mostar. She reminds them of how lucky they are to be warm and well fed and there is not a person that night who can not picture the neglect and squalor in which the unfortunates of Mostar exist daily.

She thanks them for their support tonight, for the food collection, the clothes and the money they have donated. With Carole, money is the last to be asked for, always the last to be mentioned.

A final exhortation to prayer. "This is Satan's war" she tells the hushed crowd, "only your Father in Heaven can help them now. Pray that it will end soon, that is your greatest gift of all".

It is not a pious suggestion, rather a practical solution from a practical woman who knows what Heaven is capable of when asked.

As she leaves the stage, the band strikes up and for the audience it is a welcome sound to drown the memory of her words, the pictures she has painted of desperate people just clinging to survival, hoping to exist for one more night, one more day, one more hour in the hope of salvation.

Many have died hoping and Carole remembers these as she traverses the corridor back to the temporary hospitality suite where so much is happening.

"Am I responsible for all this" she asks herself as she surveys the busy crowd. She remembers once being told by someone that he found it difficult to believe that she was just an everyday housewife and not a Minister of the Government or a Bishop of a church or the Managing Director of So and So (I) Ltd., who triggered these people to action." Maybe you should be in politics" he laughed "we need people like you. You can have my number one anytime."

Just an everyday housewife who said: please can you help, and the people of Dungarvan did.

She is brought back to reality by Seán O'Farrell who wants to congratulate her on her work. He knows about long nights and driving in the small hours.

For many of the artists this is their first contribution to Bosnia and they are delighted with the opportunity to help. The audience are beneficiaries of all the good will, and willingly play their part as they sing, clap and cheer for the duration of the programme.

As she passes the main door she sees the House Full sign and checks her watch. Nine-fifty, a magnificent evening, a value for money night which will be talked about for years.

Not all the events she is called to are like this but she is pleased with the success and the help it will bring.

And still the guests arrive, a word for each one as Tony busies himself with the committee. There is money to be counted, something at which he is skilled and he happily sorts the raffle money as Carole gratefully sips a coffee.

A word for a pressman who happens along and with luck it will end up as a few column inches somewhere.

Exhaustion is not far away as the Cork couple finally leave the lobby of the Park Hotel with Carole clutching an audio tape of a talk she gave to the schoolchildren here some months back.

She had been promised it at the time but thought it had been forgotten. Now she has a souvenir of an occasion she enjoyed very much.

As they clear the outskirts of town she plays the tape but only manages to stay awake for a few minutes as her heavy eyelids, further weighted by a comfortable seat and powerful heater finally succumb to the inevitable.

As she drifts into sleep she has a mental picture of the children at home and knows she will be with them in an hour or so.

Tony switches to a tape of Crystal Gayle - he will listen to Carole's' talk with her tomorrow evening - and to the strains of "Once in a very blue moon" he checks his seat belt again, settles in his seat and watches the needle hover near sixty.

Carole's eyes have the gritty feeling of tiredness as she stumbles in her door at home and with little ceremony she retires to bed.

A still alert Tony hopes that Sarah remembered to tape Coronation Street and he settles into the sofa with remote control in hand to complete a long and hectic day with twenty five minutes of pure Manchester escapism.

8

SPREADING THE MESSAGE

Everyone hoped that 1993 would bring a better future for the peoples of Yugoslavia but privately Carole felt that it would get much worse before it would get better.

The Serb army was the third largest in Europe and they had stocked up on munitions from Eastern Europe before the conflict started. Their own munitions industry was very advanced and made T.34 tanks for the Russian Army.

Carole was well aware of the desire in Belgrade for a greater Serbia and their hopes of linking the Serbian populations of the six republics together. Without a coastline Serbia felt isolated and unable to properly develop a tourist industry which it would hope to do in the years ahead outside of any strategic military advantage ready access to the sea would have .

The arrival of foreign visitors would give their country an acceptability in the community of Europe which it did not yet have, and there were the economic benefits to be considered as well.

They would not be able to expand their borders by peaceful means, Slovenia, Croatia and Bosnia had already let it be known that they wanted independence and freedom from the influence of Belgrade.

Their strategy then had to be a military one and they set about their task of clearing great areas of countryside of Croatian and Muslim inhabitants.

So the world learned of the practice of ethnic cleansing and for a while it did not project the horror which was hidden behind the benign expression.

All too soon it became clear what was going on but in isolated rural areas it was not possible to stop their advance. One by one the villages fell to the merciless shelling, the frontal assault, the bloody butchery and those who could get away in time never returned.

All trace of them was obliterated. Street names were changed, even gravestones substituted and soon a town bore no evidence that a Muslim or Croat community had ever existed there.

Like some evil Passover, the devils of death ravaged the land sparing only Serbian homes and even in that, mistakes were made and sometimes their own people became victims too.

Cries for help echoed around Europe, but governments did not want to know. Sunk in the torpor of their own inactivity the pleas went unanswered.

On the ground the U.N. troops did what they could but their hands were tied. The French distinguished themselves under General Morillon who had to battle not only a savage winter, and hostile local forces but had to contend with political disapproval at home.

The people of the world sat up and took notice. General Courage had made a stand for right and for decency and they were proud. But it was a small victory in a widespread war and elsewhere the people continued to die in their thousands from cold and hunger or as innocent bystanders in a conflict not of their making.

The people of Ireland heard the pleas, conveyed by a variety of aid agencies which channelled their efforts to Bosnia.

In January 1993 Carole launched a food appeal in Dunne's Stores in Douglas which was renewed several times in the next year. At last the people had an outlet for their goodwill and the aid flooded in.

Irish people can readily identify with hunger and whether it is a child on Patrick's Bridge or a woman in Bosnia they can not pass blindly by.

Whether it was the plight of the hungry, the thought of women being made homeless or the cry of the children matters little, every call was answered and the shopping trolleys filled.

Carole was greatly encouraged but not surprised for she had worked also through the Croatian conflict and had seen generosity in action. Each person's contribution might only be a drop, but enough of them would make an ocean.

So Carole and Áine set themselves up as the two anchors, one in Bosnia, the other in Ireland and in between was the chain of which the people would be individual links.

It was a practical view of a simple concept and it was to work beautifully.

They were starting from scratch and for the moment would confine themselves to the immediate Munster area. Carole put advertisements in the Cork Examiner, Southern Star and her own local Carrigdhoun Weekly and enlisted the help of 89 F.M.'s Alf McCarthy, Stevie Bolger, Pat O'Donovan and Ger McLoughlin. County Sound, the local commercial radio station agreed to help through Patricia Messenger and the appeal was launched.

Carole enlisted the support of family and friends to bring the food to the warehouse and soon the stacks were beginning to grow. All the time she spent on the campaign now was active with no time-consuming hours sitting uselessly around a table.

This is how the other volunteers wished it as well and they made a good team. Her family worked with her and one of the most consistent helpers was her father. Tony and the children would help when there was a push on and it was good to see all the family working and spending time together.

Companies donated food and hospitals gave medical supplies which they would not use in time or which had just exceeded their use by dates but would still be well within the safety limits. The shelf life of medical supplies in Mostar Hospital was short, such was the throughput of patients.

Everyone was glad to get the goods and Dr. Martinovic understood the conditions under which they were collected though he too drew the line when he saw the consignment of biscuits come in from the U.S. dated 1978.

It took about a month to put that first container load together and everyone was proud when a week into March it finally pulled away from the warehouse bound for Mostar.

Inside were fifteen pallets laden with food and four pallets of medical supplies. The rest of the space was full of blankets, sheets and clothes and Carole thought as she supervised the closing and sealing of the doors that it was a consignment of which everyone could feel proud.

Some of the proudest amongst the little group of people who saw it off were their own children. Even Kristian had soon learned to seal boxes with tape and it was funny to see the six year old instruct a grown man in the use of the tape dispenser.

Carole had always encouraged their children to help. She felt it was an exercise in sharing and she hoped the experience would have a beneficial effect later on.

It was also her hope that if roles were reversed and it was our people who were dying on the hillsides that there would be some country to take an interest in us and send some help.

She was reminded again of how unselfish and broadminded she had found the Irish people each time she had asked for help. She had never expected it to be otherwise but she was reminded of articles she had read in the paper about how we are reputed to be selective in who we help.

She had announced publicly to everyone that people of all creeds and none would benefit and if the plight of any one ethnic group were highlighted above another it was that of the Muslim women who had suffered most.

Now there would be some recompense from the Irish people, an attempt to say sorry on behalf of the world community. The material goods would go some way towards making amends.

Those who had worked on it knew that the tins of beans and spaghetti they had packed would be the only food between some of the people there and starvation.

They knew that the tissues and toilet rolls represented a little luxury for the people, that the chocolate bars and crayons and colouring books would be received by the children there as expensive computer games would be by children in Ireland.

The task was to convey this to the Irish people, that their contribution would be of immediate and vital benefit to the population there.

Determined to see the supplies safely in the hands of the people who needed them the most, and in an effort to help Áine with the distribution Carole decided to travel to Mostar to coincide with the arrival of the container. In a sense she would work her passage as she would bring medical supplies on the plane with her. Items which she would prefer to see transferred from hand to hand and which had a short life.

She assembled twenty one pieces and enlisted the support of Fr. Seán O'Driscoll, Chaplain to the Carrigaline Community School to go with her.

While they were there Áine suggested visiting a small village in the mountains of which she had heard very disquieting reports. They found appalling hardship with stories of a massacre, deprivation and hunger not seen outside of Africa.

There and then she committed herself to being back there in two weeks and came home a very angry and determined woman. She alerted R.T.E. in Cork and appeared on the Late News on Network 2 still choking with rage and frustration that people could inflict these horrors on each other in 1993.

The response was huge, and true to her word she was back in the village in a few weeks with the much needed supplies. Her decision to go out that first time had paid off and she learned valuable lessons about the practical handling of supplies and got to know the conditions on the ground there.

On her return, Carole redoubled her efforts. She was getting more and more enquiries and invitations to speak at meetings and functions. People would make contact with her to arrange a once-off fund-raising event or appeal but invariably the groups stayed the distance and continued to supply goods, money and more importantly prayers for peace.

Their efforts were often instrumental in keeping people alive.

Everywhere she went, Carole would talk about the human misery and suffering which is the daily lot of the people of Bosnia. Whenever she got an opportunity she would produce photographs of the bombed city of Mostar, the wrecked bridges, the single cold tap which was the only source of water supply for a city block.

Áine had given her a heavy piece of shrapnel about three inches long which had been removed from a young girls back without the benefit of an anaesthetic. Seeing this invariably horrified people, but it brought home to them in a very practical way the realities of life in the war conditions of Mostar.

People would linger over the photographs or the shrapnel or the Croatian rosary beads which she brought with her and she would tell them of the atrocities being committed against the civilian population.

Always, before she would finish, Carole would talk of the need for prayer and stop the war. "This is a satanic War" she would tell her listeners and beseech them to say even one Our Father per day.

Man cannot stop this war, she would tell them, only a concerted campaign of prayer to bring the leaders to their senses.

In March she was invited to a day of Prayer for Peace to be held on a hilltop in the foothills of the Comeraghs on Easter Monday. A good deal of promotion had gone into the event which it was hoped would draw a large crowd from the surrounding counties.

Some short time previously, Susan McHugh had founded the new Peace Movement in Ireland and it was decided to ask people to sign a petition for peace. The list of signatories would then be sent to Susan McHugh and Áine Burke in Bosnia as a sign of the people's solidarity with them.

Almost a thousand people turned up to the climb and in the driving rain a prayer vigil was held on the top of the mountain.

Carole was always in demand to speak, to explain, to ask people to be generous. There were never enough nights in the week or hours in the day to do what needed to be done. She was invited to speak to the members of Bishopstown Rotary Club and in the rarefied atmosphere of the Cork Captains of Industry she told them that they too must be generous. "You have made your money", she said, "and it is now time to share some of it with the people who have nothing".

They did and between them all, came close to filling a container.

At this stage Bosnia was getting saturation coverage and was on everyone's lips. All over the estates in Cork fund-raising events were held. In villages and towns around Munster card-drives, dances, sales of work, fetes and table quizzes were held and as a result the supplies built steadily in the warehouse.

Hearing Carole's plea on the radio one evening, Edel, a twelve year old Cork girl decided to take action. As she listened with her mother to Carole on the radio, they spoke about how difficult it must have been for the children there.

Without any further reference to her mother Edel decided to put her plan in train. The following evening a man came to the door and told her mother that the use of the local hall had been approved.

Her mother did not know what he was talking about and it took an explanation on Edel's arrival home to clear up the matter. On her own initiative she had sought the use of the school hall for a jumble sale and was canvassing around the neighbourhood for toys, books and any items which would be of interest.

She donated her own dolls' house as the first prize in the raffle. With the willing help of her family and friends she held the jumble sale and lodged over £120 into the account.

It was incidents like that which inspired Carole to keep going, but she never doubted that the goodwill of the people was always behind her.

There were many other individual acts of kindness which meant so much to her, and the people of Bosnia. One day she was approached by a businessman who told her that if she filled a container he would supply the cost of transport.

It lifted a major responsibility from Carole's shoulders not to have to find that money and all her energies could be channelled into filling the container and getting it on the road.

Containers were now leaving every two or three weeks and reaching the places most in need. It saddened Carole to hear that Ulog, the little village in the mountains was again deserted having once more come under attack, this time by the Muslims.

The plans she had to rebuild the village and re-equip the houses with kitchen utensils and furniture had to be put on hold and she sometimes wonders whether the villagers will ever return to their homes again. For many months during the worst of the fighting, the village was inaccessible but her commitment to help rebuild the village after the war is still strong with Carole.

Áine's home county of Galway also sent supplies. She had spoken there the previous year and Carole was asked to come up and renew the message. She spoke at the masses on Saturday evening and Sunday morning and an organisation was set up.

As a result of that, almost a full container load of supplies arrived to the warehouse where it was topped up and sent on to Mostar. The West as usual was wide awake and continued from then on to send substantial supplies to the warehouse in Cork. Support came from the most unlikely sources and it never failed to amaze Carole, the people who contributed money and material aid, organised fund-raising events or promoted the cause in a particular area. Supplies came from as far away as Northern Ireland and several groups there sent regular shipments to Cork. Very often Carole did not know much of the history of a contribution, knowing only that a lodgement was made in a particular area of the country as a result of some fund-raising event large or small.

Everything was needed, everything was appreciated, everything was sent to Bosnia. There would never be enough but Carole was delighted with what was being done and proud that she could be the one to co-ordinate the product of peoples effort, time and goodwill.

The generosity of the Irish people, as well as Carole's own work and ability to motivate others was recognised in January 1994 when she was the recipient of the Evening Echo/Southern Advertising/Jury's Hotel Person of the Month Award. Surprised that she was nominated, let alone a winner, Carole was pleased to accept the award from Maurice Gubbins of The Cork Examiner.

Proudly displayed in her living room, the polished wood keepsake is a constant reminder to her of the responsibilities she assumed to the people of Bosnia. Practical as ever, Carole appreciated as much the column inches which appeared in the following days papers, under the headline "Carole Wants War Trials", which gave her Appeal further publicity and drew more people to the warehouse with donations of aid and offers of help.

Paying tribute to Carole, Maurice Gubbins described her operation in the warehouse as "one of the few voluntary production lines in the world." He was even more impressed by her skill as a communicator, and "how she could convey the horror of the war without glorying in or over-dramatising the excesses being committed there."

1994 also saw Carole acknowledged in her own town. At the annual Carrigdhoun Weekly Awards Ceremony, Carole was presented with the special category prize for her humanitarian work in Bosnia.

Not many prophets are accepted in their own land, but Carrigaline is proud of Carole, proud of her work and the honour she brings to the town, and in turn Carole is pleased that her work is appreciated.

In years to come, her awards, together with the many other mementoes and photographs she has collected, will be items to be treasured, and will bring back warm memories, but, while war rages in Bosnia and while people go to bed hungry, they can only be a spur to greater efforts.

Carole receives the Carrigdhoun Weekly Special Category Award from
Sean O'Halloran, Ballygarvan Concrete, Sponsors.
Also included is Ken O'Day, organiser
Photo courtesy of Carrigdhoun Weekly

9

Testimony of Kemal & Kadira

They have been sitting in the bus on this bridge for several hours now and the temperature outside is 35ºC. What it has reached inside the bus they can only guess but no one will want to complain. All are still in a high state of tension, the children are tired and hungry, the old people ready to collapse.

They have reached the relative sanctuary of Croatia but even here there is no guarantee of safety for a Muslim. Serb vengeance extends beyond the boundaries of Yugoslavia and it will be some time before Kemal and Kadira will feel truly outside the clutches of the people who have so wrecked their lives. Croatia has been good to the Muslims, having given sanctuary to several hundred thousand of them for the duration of the war. They have been fed, housed and educated, and Croatia helped arm the Muslims in Bosnia.

Kemal and Kadira have still only travelled less than sixty miles and they have been on the road for over twelve hours. There is still a half-hours' drive to Zagreb but there is no telling how long that will take. However the immediate danger is past but getting the necessary travel documents from the United Nations could take a month or more.

Kemal and Kadira and the rest of the family who have accompanied them are glad to have made it, to have finally shaken off the constant tension, the constant threat, the ever present mental torture which had been their lives for a year and a half since the outbreak of war.

134

Kemal can still remember the night when the Serb thugs arrived in his town and started to cause mayhem in the streets. They fired guns, they threatened the locals, they beat innocent people; It seemed that they were there only to provoke trouble.

No one knew who they were, they just arrived in the night and like Hitler's thugs in the 'thirties they set about creating an atmosphere of terror.

In Sarajevo they did the same. Thugs ferried in from a distance and after forty eight hours they had the city in a turmoil from which it has not recovered since.

Within days those who had not volunteered in the Serb Army were fired from their jobs, ostensibly because business had slumped and redundancies were necessary but significantly no Serbs were left go.

In those early days Muslims and Croats were asked to sign pledges of allegiance in order to hold their jobs but eventually this was not even enough, and more and more were pushed out of employment. Ethnic cleansing in practice: no job meant no home, no welfare payments meant no survival, no prospects, no point in staying around.

Kemal dreaded what might happen to his family, but he took some comfort from the fact that he had lengthy service and his firm was not doing too badly. Fearfully through the months they saw many of their friends lose their jobs, their livelihoods, their total existence. Without a welfare system it was work or starve, and the Serbs relied on hunger to clear a town of Muslims and Croats. It was ethnic cleansing at its cleanest, skilfully enforced with no visible intimidation.

But physical intimidation played a part too for those who could not be bullied or threatened in any other way. The Serbs are master of the late-night knock at the door, the brandishing of weapons, the senseless beatings and the mysterious disappearance of whole families.

Early in the war Serb soldiers would invade a household and force the men to lower their trousers. Those whom they found to have been circumcised would be shot where they stood in front of a horrified family, once more victims of their religious beliefs.

In the summer Kemal applied for his two weeks holidays as usual and he was told that he need not return. Dry-mouthed, weak-kneed shock was all he could register as he realised that the war had once more caught up with his family. Not content with having lost one son - to a safer land they hoped - they were now to become victims themselves.

Kadira was also in employment and when she too was told not to return to her job, their whole world had collapsed about them.

For as long as they could they struggled on, but they were becoming less desirable citizens by the day, at least in the eyes of the Serbs who administered their town. There was a time when Muslims formed the largest ethnic group but on the eventual collapse of Communism more and more Serbs had been brought in from the outlying villages to slowly build the Serb population to a majority.

With that majority came power and for the Serbian regime that means absolute power with absolute domination and corruption. More and more houses needed to be found for these migrants, more jobs and more land.

These came from the departing Muslim and Croat population who were glad to escape with their lives and eventually were only too willing to sign away their property and give a written guarantee never to return in exchange for the necessary travel documents.

If they had no property to give, they were nonentities, cast into the gutter, abandoned and forgotten, lucky not to have found a place in a mass grave with a bullet in the head or a bayonet across the throat.

The only thing approaching a welfare system in Bosnia was the concentration camp and people soon learned that not even subsistence levels of food were available there. Their only alternative was to try for a visa, but while they might succeed in gaining permission to leave Bosnia/ Hercegovina a problem would inevitably arise in trying to enter Croatia without a written undertaking from some foreign government that they would accept them and underwrite education, health and housing cost. Croatia was already groaning under the weight of a variety of refugees and did what they could for allcomers. Without family or friends abroad what chance had they of getting over this almost insurmountable obstacle?

As their savings dwindled, used to keep body and soul together, so too did their chances of retaining their home. Kemal helped his cousins till their small patch of land but the daily round trip of some miles became increasingly hazardous with police, military and paramilitary patrols and checkpoints seemingly everywhere.

Worst of all were the Cetniks who were capable of the greatest cruelties at little or even no provocation. An encounter with them as many found out often ended in a one way trip.

The cost of living had soared with a thriving black market. Often it was the old who suffered most with their meagre monthly pensions barely enough to buy one packet of cigarettes or a litre of oil for cooking.

The only ones who had money were the soldiers who seemed to have a limitless supply and kept the price of everything high.

Eventually, Kemal and Kadira could take the pressure no longer. The final straw had come when they had to surrender their home to a Serb Army Officer. All they had worked for all their lives was coming apart. Family scattered, their home gone and not even the right to walk the streets in peace.

They retreated to their cousins in the country where they took turns at tending the land, sometimes fearful to come outside even for that.

With difficulty they made contact with friends abroad to ask them to petition a friendly government to give them the necessary undertaking which would satisfy the Croatians to allow them to travel through their country. No one entered Croatia without being able to guarantee that they could travel on to another country. They already had a huge population of refugees and could take no more.

That undertaking had to be received before ever they thought of requesting travel documents from the Serb authorities.

In Ireland a woman from Cork called Carole Wiley was contacted by relations of the family to help smooth the path for their exit from Bosnia. Without the required guarantee their chances of getting to Croatia are nil and time is running out.

Carole readily agrees to help and rings the Department of Foreign Affairs making use of the contacts she made the previous Spring. They are polite and helpful but there are channels to be gone through and formalities to be completed before they can act. Refugee Trust, Dail Deputies, people of influence are all petitioned. Through the Summer contact is made with Bosnia, information is exchanged and dates of birth and other statistics are established. Carole also contacts the U.N. in Zagreb with the necessary information and after several other meetings with government officials, passports are issued.

Approval is given for Kemal and Kadira to be included in the next group of refugees arriving into the country and the joyful word is passed back to Bosnia.

Kemal and Kadira are ecstatic, though their happiness is tempered by fear for the friends and family to be left behind.

Knowing that the worst is yet to come they apply to leave Serbian controlled Bosnia/Hercegovina.

Each day they would wait in fear of being arrested by some uniformed Serb. They had nothing to hide but they were Muslims in what was fast becoming a totally Serb town. For months they had seen the Friday convoys roll out bearing those "fortunates" who had completed the formalities of handing over their property and finally accepting the inevitable.

Not all who boarded the buses made it safely to their eventual destination. A succession of check-points took their toll and very often people were taken from the buses never to be seen again.

Now, as they sat in the oven-like atmosphere in the broiling sun, Kemal recalled the last few months of sheer hell as they tried to survive. Even though they were not confined they seemed to live the same day to day existence of the condemned prisoner in his cell.

They were as confined to the house as if there were a round the clock guard. Each night as they went to bed they never knew if they would be alive the following morning. Kemal would prop the front door with a plank, to keep out unwanted callers, but he knew that this was purely a psychological advantage, a cosmetic exercise for the rest of the family only. He knew that if the uniforms wished to gain entry a few well placed rifle butts would have the door down in no time.

They had electricity intermittently, an occasional water supply, a telephone when it worked and some financial reserves since before the war but they knew that they could not hold out indefinitely.

Each time he moved back or forth between home and his cousins before finally moving to stay with them, Kemal knew he took a great chance of being picked up or worse still being shot on sight. There was no Mosque or church in which to find shelter, all had long since been destroyed by the Serbs.

Then in December, the worst happened. As with so many Christian or Muslim feasts, there was a huge round-up to coincide with Christmas and Kemal was lodged in a concentration camp. He blocks out the memory of the conditions there but his experiences in the month he was in the camp will stay with him all of his life. Just days after he and others were freed, the camp was closed and the remaining prisoners were sent to the front-line without weapons.

For them it was certain death but an alternative might have been the execution squad on the edge of a pit filled with quicklime.

Their house was raided often, looking for fugitives and very often the soldiers would steal what they wanted without reprimand from those in charge. On such visits to households where a member of the family was wanted for some reason, they would taunt the families with stories of what would happen if the person were caught. The Serbs can be quite inventive under such circumstances and they do not always exaggerate.

Many families, unable to resist the pressure any longer, finally submitted to the inevitable and booked a seat on one of the Friday convoys. In the early days when there were many Muslims and Croats in the town there could be up to twenty buses in the convoy, each packed to capacity. This would mean anything up to a thousand people would leave by that route alone each week.

As the Croat and Muslim numbers in the town dwindled, so the convoys got shorter and today there are only two buses going. But the size of the convoy meant nothing in terms of safety. Once a friend of Kemal's was on the last bus of twenty as it departed for the relative safety of Croatia.

Their guide promised that they would try to avoid Cetnik checkpoints along the way as they had sustained heavy losses in the war zone that day and would be looking for revenge. A busload of Muslims would make an ideal reprisal. If they board the bus, do not annoy them, their guide told them. If they ask questions, answer them quickly. The fate of everyone rested on complete co-operation.

The convoy was stopped at many checkpoints along the way and passed with relative ease. Unfortunately one of those checkpoints was manned by Cetniks and as predicted they were in an angry mood.

They gave vent to their anger as they rough-handled the passengers in their search getting them to take off even shoes and socks to show they were not hiding any money, gold or other valuables. When you left Serbian control you took little or nothing with you.

Their Serb driver noted the unusually strong hostility amongst the Cetniks and pleaded with his passengers to be fully co-operative. As the vehicle in front of them sped away, they were left to face the anger of the soldiers alone.

They surround the bus in mob fashion beating the sides frightening more than the children. Some have guns at the ready, others toss hand-grenades from hand to hand suggestively.

Their intent is clear and the passengers dive to the floor. Their driver pleads for them and despite being a Serb he is threatened with a bullet in the head. Wisely he shuts up, keeps his head down and stays in his seat.

They know they have only minutes to live and each prepares for the worst. Suddenly around the bend comes a police car with lights flashing and sirens blaring. The Cetniks are distracted long enough for the scared driver to put his foot to the floor and speed away to leave the police and the Cetniks to argue it out. It had been close.

They are too late to rejoin the convoy so they return to their town once more. Next Friday they will not be the last in the convoy, the driver will see to that, and will eventually make the Croatian border safely.

Kemal and Kadira have been spared that particular trauma and consider their present predicament in the hothouse-like bus a mild inconvenience by comparison. They think of the dwindling numbers of Muslim's left behind. Those with no one to work for them abroad, those who cannot get visas, those with no leverage, no property to barter, what will become of them?

They were due to travel last week, but a last minute bureaucratic hitch eventually prevented that. In Ireland, out of contact, Carole was worried by the delay and it was a long week to the following Friday and the next convoy. Not knowing what caused the delay she worried each day and prayed regularly for their safety. Eventually, at their second attempt they boarded the bus and were on their way.

Kemal looks around the bus and reviews the wide variety of passengers. They are young and old, male and female, sick and well. All types except men of military age who are in one of the several armies available to them, gone abroad to avoid compulsory military service with the Serbs, or are already gone to an early grave.

They have been on the road for over thirteen hours now, with few facilities available to them. What little food they had had, they have eaten. They have used their water sparingly but soon they will be with relations who will have free passage around town.

They have mixed feelings about the prospect of living in a foreign country. They know they will be safe there, have another chance of a decent lifestyle, but there will be language difficulties and it will not be Bosnia. Everyone pines for their homeland, if not for the people who have made life there impossible.

Kemal takes a moment to reflect on how things could have gone so badly wrong in such a short space of time and once more concludes that the ordinary folk who up to the engineered disturbances of March 1992, could have lived in peace, would have been happy to continue in peaceful coexistence if they had been allowed.

But here they are homeless, and, for the moment at least, stateless, without possessions, but they are lucky enough to have their family still intact. All will be united one day, they know, and that day is something to look forward to.

As the evening sun sinks into the west throwing a golden mantle over the beautiful summer countryside the buses begin moving again. Soon they will be among friends and they will have a chance to relax. The first step in a journey into an uncertain future.

As Bosnia/Hercegovina slips further and further behind into the gathering dusk, Kemal and Kadira wonder if they will ever see their country again. Could things ever change sufficiently that they would come back? For them, never. Theirs is a Serb town now and whatever settlement is arrived as they know will preclude them returning to the home they have worked so hard for. Perhaps elsewhere in Bosnia, if there will be a Bosnia in the future. It has grown so small in a year and a half that they wonder if anything could be salvaged for the Muslims of the country.

All that is for the future, tonight they will sleep reasonably peacefully in their beds. They have friends to transact their public business for them and as soon as their visas are granted they will be gone. They know that they are tolerated rather than welcomed by the State of Croatia, which is already maintaining a huge number of refugees from Bosnia/Hercegovina and they will linger as short as possible. Anything is better than what they have left and the people of their new country, they know, are renowned for their welcome.

Soon they will know at first hand if it is true.

10

MINDING THE STORE

There could never be too much food in the warehouse. Sometimes it can be overloaded with clothes and it takes a share of several containers to shift them all. Carole likes to send a balanced container including about one third each of food, clothes and medical items. If it is high summer, the need for clothes is less, but there is always a winter looming and Carole dislikes to stop the continuity of collection.

But food and medicines are necessary all year round and there could never be too much. Which is why this weekend, Carole has, with the help of her volunteers and the local supermarkets, decided to hold a food appeal.

She dreads the weekend, such will be the pressure and hard work, but it should be worth it all with a container on its way before the week is out. The appeal has to be planned weeks in advance. Carole has long ago learnt the old military maxim, "Time spent in reconnaissance is never time wasted". If her group is before the public she wants to make it worthwhile and nothing annoys her more than a badly planned event which yields little. If there's pain and public exposure there should be gain.

The appeal will last three days, starting at nine o'clock each morning, running through to 9 p.m. on Thursday and Friday and six o'clock on Saturday. She dreads to think how her back will feel by Saturday evening or how large her ankles will be, but it's for a good cause, it's for Bosnia.

She made out her rota a week ago and barring an epidemic of tonsillitis, the collection points should be well staffed all weekend. As she eases the car out the driveway, she flicks through her mental checklist and hopes all is in order.

She has been up since seven thirty getting things organised at home and Caroline, their faithful and reliable friend and babysitter, arrived an hour later to take over for the next few days. It would be unfair to Tony and the children to load them with extra duties or leave them less than well catered for, so she will delve into her personal kitty to pay for her substitute, though as sometimes happens Caroline will make her work in the Wiley household her contribution to Bosnia Relief.

She delivers the children to school and then goes straight to Dunne's Stores in Douglas which will be her home almost continually for the next three days. In fact she will spend almost thirty six hours on the premises or close to it and another three or four in the warehouse. That amounts to a normal week's work in the industrial sector, but will be dismissed by those who don't think about such things as "a little bit of effort".

As she pulls into the store car park at five minutes to nine she sees there is already a queue of ten or eleven people anxious to do their weeks shopping before the store gets really busy. She checks in with Manager, Joe Dukes, assures him everything is in order at her end and sets up the stand in the main lobby to show the photographs of Mostar Hospital and people receiving aid.

Joe Dukes, Dunnes Stores and their other local managers have been a huge asset to Carole's campaign. Their help and co-operation has been total and through their assistance and the generosity of the Irish people, many pallets of food have been loaded for Bosnia.

The staff of Dunnes Stores are personally generous too, bringing items from home, making collections with which to buy food and Joe has been able to top-up many a pallet for Carole through the contributions of the representatives and sales-people of supplier companies.

Today the constant rota of helpers will hand leaflets to the incoming shoppers asking for their support and detailing the list of items which are most needed, easiest to pack and transport

"Minding the Store . . . during a fund-raising event in Dunnes Stores in Douglas, Cork. These range from regular food appeals to packing groceries for customers in return for a contribution to the Carole Wiley Bosnia Appeal."

Carole Wiley with Joe Dukes Manager of the Dunnes Stores Branch in Douglas.

and will be of most value in the deprived homes of Bosnia. The list is comprehensive and the items range in price from nineteen pence to ten or fifteen pounds, so no one need feel left out.

Jan's husband Malcolm, and her friends Dee and Sharon, both from Carole's immediate neighbourhood have agreed to operate the first shift until eleven o'clock and both are experienced and need no instructions. Malcolm will take away the donated items in his delivery van to the warehouse and Carole feels it very important that there should be no clutter in the store.

The leaflets are handed out to the incoming shoppers, some of whom stop and chat with the collectors about Bosnia and the dreadful conditions there. As a rule, people know very little about the various factions involved in the fighting or what little political process there is, and are less than concerned about them. They invariably ask about the people, the weather conditions and Medjugorje, where many people are anxious to return on pilgrimage.

A local councillor greets her and enquires about the appeal. Carole has little time to be in contact with local politics and wonders how she would perform if she were involved. Certainly in the Dáil she would have her own opinions, and even now she has her own views on how the people of Ireland could be served even better. She would be anxious to speak her mind on every subject which affected the people, and would set herself realistic goals for which she would staunchly fight and achieve. She answers the councillor's questions and he assures her of his support telling her to get in touch if there is anything he can do.

More and more customers are coming to the store, accepting leaflets and depositing a variety of goods in the appeal trolleys. The pile is growing and soon Malcolm will have to deliver to the warehouse. Before that they decide to have their elevenses, and in rota go to Teazers restaurant for coffee.

Even there she is approached by people who congratulate her on her work, wish her well and promise their help on a limited basis. She fills one or two vacant spots on the rota for Saturday and returns to her vigil, this time with two of the sisters from the local Sacred Heart Convent.

Sr. Philomena and Sr. Imelda have collected before so they know the routine. Carole loves to see the sisters involved and they in turn like to be able to give practical help to the people of Bosnia.

A youth with blue hair in the Mohican style approaches her and for a moment she is a little concerned by this apparition in black leather, shining studs and hanging safety pins. He asks politely for a leaflet and Carole smiles uncertainly as he takes it. He disappears among the aisles and fifteen minutes later he is on his way out with a laden trolley. He takes a small bag of messages from the top and Carole beings to thank him for his generosity when he eases his trolley among the already full ones beside her.

She is stunned, stammers her thanks at his retreating back and not for the first time chides herself for being surprised at the source of a windfall. She thought she had learned never to judge the book by the cover, indeed never to judge at all, but we seem to have got very fixed ideas about particular types of people.

She finds a public phone, checks in with 89 Fm with whom she is to do a short interview and in minutes is on the air. News of the appeal will be carried on both local stations over the next few days and will be a tremendous boost. She is glad the public never seem to tire of learning about Bosnia and she knows that the majority do not approve of the seeming inactivity of Western governments in trying to find a solution.

On her return, Joe Dukes comes over and they tour the aisles to check on the stock from which people are likely to select their purchases for Bosnia. It is noticeable that on the days of the food appeal certain lines will clear very quickly, and have to be topped up when they seem to be low. Joe has long since learned what will be in demand and often orders in extra stock ahead in anticipation of demand.

If a particular item is likely to be sold out, Joe will have further stock delivered from another branch across the city and every effort will be made to keep the shoppers happy and the appeal as successful as possible. It is a busy morning and time goes quickly, so it comes as a surprise to Carole that it is on the brink of lunch time.

Jan and Sharon come in to take over the trolleys so Carole takes the opportunity to go for lunch. She has arranged to meet Tony at Teazers Restaurant in Douglas Court for lunch. She will let him know how the appeal is going and give him some details of things to be checked at home. He will also be in touch with home during the afternoon to see that the children have got there safely and that they are not taking advantage of Caroline's good nature.

It will be one of the few hours they will spend together this weekend and they are glad of the opportunity of catching up on family matters. Carole likes to eat at Teazers who have been very good to the volunteers during the various Bosnia appeals.

Carole, who eats little in the middle of the day opts for soup and a sandwich but Tony has the Chicken Kiev, a favourite of his. He tells her that some of the staff heard her on 89 Fm and it had generated a bit of good-humoured banter in the office as they referred to Carole as Mrs. Bosnia.

Carole asks Tony if he will look in on her parents in Roche's Stores where the appeal is also being conducted, to see that they have no difficulties. It is not long since they collected in Quinnsworth and they have found from experience that it is difficult to keep three stores serviced at the one time. Carole's father will ferry the donations to the warehouse as they pile up, which is one more difficult area covered.

Lunch time, the fastest hour in the day, goes quickly and Tony returns to work, Carole to her appeal. The women at the trolleys are happy with progress so Carole does a quick tour of the shelves to assess stocks. Jan has to leave to pick up both her own children and Carole's so pending the arrival of the four o'clock shift, Carole stands by the trolleys.

An elderly lady, obviously of retirement age approaches Carole and slips a note into her hand saying it is a small donation towards her work. Carole dreads such occasions because she knows the kind of sacrifice which is involved in such contributions. She looks at the note and sees it is ten pounds. She is now torn between trying to dissuade the woman from such a large donation at the possible risk of offending her, and accepting gracefully knowing it represents a considerable portion of her weekly budget.

Carole takes a deep breath and for her own peace of mind asks the woman if she can afford to give so much.

"The war is in my sitting room every evening" said the woman, "and I want to do something for the people there. You are my link with them and now I can go home in peace knowing I have done something positive." Carole asks her to continue to pray that the war will soon end and they part company.

Later, one of the staff tells Carole that the woman's purchases were sausages and beans and that they may well have been for her Sunday lunch. Carole remembers the woman's remark about being a link and subsequently uses it during her talks. She is reminded again of the responsibility she feels that every penny given by the public should be used wisely and accounted for later. People in Ireland have big hearts and it would not be fair to make excessive demands on their generosity. If the goods are given free, they should be distributed free. They are given by all for the benefit of all. This could well have been the woman's grocery money for the weekend and her gesture could, at the least, have represented a reduced standard of living for the next week.

Yes, her aid goes to all sections of the population in Bosnia, she assures another woman, and not for the first time tells someone that if she ever felt it did not benefit Muslim, Croat and even Serbs in need, she would give up. What mother buys sweets for just one of her children, she tells the woman, everyone has to be remembered when she goes to town. There can be no favouritism.

There is a lull in activity during what for most people is teatime and the volunteers take the opportunity to have coffee and a sandwich. It will get busy again by about seven with the last two hours hectic as people shop for the weekend.

Carole's back is beginning to feel the strain of the constant standing so she again tours the store to inspect the shelves and ease the pain where she injured herself in the garden some years ago. Enthusiastic at everything she does, she had set about rearranging her garden one Saturday. She dug up shrubs to be moved elsewhere and typically tried to do too much in one day. Moving a particularly large Hebe she felt her back pinch and she knew she had done some damage. Ever since it has been a weak link though she knows when to take it easy. Her trips to Mostar have taken their toll too, and she finds her back very tired after the strain of wearing a heavy flak-jacket for hours on end. The jacket is as much a psychological protection as physical and it helps her family cope with knowing she is in the war zone.

By eight o'clock they have shifted about forty trolley loads to the warehouse and she resolves that if she is not delayed too long by the straggler shoppers she will make a quick run to the Marina Commercial Park and do some of the sorting. The staff are busily stocking the shelves for the following day. Friday is one of the busiest days of the week and they will need every minute to keep everything under control. The Dunne's stores staff have been very good to the appeal and on the last occasion, they gave that weeks proceeds of their social club contributions to the fund.

As well as that many make donations of food purchased in the store, making their combined contribution a very considerable one. Finally at nine twenty five, Carole helps Malcolm and his father and Carole's brother Declan to load the last of the items in the van to take them to the warehouse. Carole travels with Declan and they all work for about half an hour to get the items into some sort of order.

Finally, tiredness, hunger and the prospect of two more tough days send them home and Carole is glad to see the inside of 45 Liosbourne. Tony has anticipated her need for a cup of coffee and a comfortable chair, and she luxuriates in front of the large fire for a few minutes to acclimatise. It is obvious Caroline has been busy, but there are some items Carole needs to attend to herself. She inspects the last of the homework, supervises prayers and sends Mark and Audrey to bed. Kristian has been gone for some time but she suspects he is not asleep yet.

She discusses her school project with Sarah and advises her on how to go about it, promising help where her daughter might need it. Finally Sarah too retires to bed and she and Tony settle down for the last programme of the evening. As so often happens she begins to nod in the warmth and quiet of the comfortable living room. She wakes to Tony's gentle shaking, but before she can become fully alert she decides to go to bed, leaving him to secure the house and see that Deefer, their dog, is settled for the night.

The seven thirty alarm will come all too quickly and in the meantime she will take advantage of whatever rest she can get. Sleepily, she adds her own final prayers to those she said with the children and finally drifts into a sleep she hopes will not be disturbed by nightmares of a young girl with impossibly brown eyes recovering from shrapnel wounds, strapped to a hospital bed in Mostar.

11

NOT EVERYONE AGREES

One morning in September 1993 the phone rings. There is rarely a morning when the phone does not ring a dozen times and those calls generate more phone-time later. The real winners are the phone company who have just put up their charges again.

A lady from a town forty miles away who has contributed to a collection is concerned that the Croatian side is becoming aggressive and expansionist. Up to now reports of the fighting have been mainly about Serb advances, shelling and street fighting.

Now there are reports of fighting between Muslims and Croats, the two former allies who came together in common cause against the excesses of the Serbian Army and the Cetnik irregulars. There are suggestions that the Croats are holding up an aid convoy destined for the Muslim quarter in Mostar. Arms had been found on a previous convoy destined for the Muslims and the locals are not taking any chances on this occasion. After everything is checked the trucks are released but it does demonstrate the volatility of conditions in the area.

Carole does not try to explain the politics of the region, the combined resources of R.T.E., B.B.C. and I.T.V. have been trying to do that for years and even they have difficulty sometimes working it out. Instead she concentrates on what she herself is trying to do, Áine's work in Bosnia and the goodwill which has built up towards the Áine and Carole Fund.

No, the lady persists, I want to know if we're backing the Croatian Army, the Croatian people and helping the military effort.

Carole assures her that all the aid which is sent out arrives in Mostar, and Zagreb and it's distribution is supervised there by Áine and by herself when she can fly out. She explains how the food and clothes are distributed to needy families both Muslim and Christian and to those of no religion at all.

She explains how the medical supplies are distributed around the hospitals, how the medical staff do not differentiate among patients and that even a wounded Serb soldier in the hospital will benefit from what is sent out.

But the woman is persistent, she has heard stories and wants them checked. No amount of first hand reports from Bosnia will satisfy her and suddenly a great weariness comes over Carole at the futility of it all.

Why can she not get the woman to understand that it is the people of all sides who are suffering. That cold and hunger know no political boundaries, that children of all religions need some security in life and that ten families who had had their own homes and are now thankful for a communal cowshed should not have to watch their children suffer from lack of medicine.

Her eyes fill with tears and a sob escapes her. How can she tell the woman politely that her call should be directed to those who are doing nothing about the concentration camp of Europe. That governments have stood cynically by and watched Yugoslavia tear itself apart because they had no strategic interests there.

If the country had welcomed American companies and British Investment, French Technology and German Computer Systems over the last fifty years instead of wallowing in the stagnation of communist policies there would now be F.16's in the skies, Allied troops armed with the best of Western Military technology in the streets and the war criminals awaiting trial.

If there, had been sand instead of heather, oil instead of wine, gold instead of coal the West would have sat up and taken notice. The American dominated U.N. would have put teeth in their resolutions instead of vacillating for two years with talk of another Vietnam.

There was no difficulty in getting out of Kuwait, no hesitation about going in in the first place, and there is not a resident of Mostar who has not lamented "If only we had oil".

The woman is still looking for explanations, but nothing will satisfy her. Her mind is made up. Nothing will change it.

Wearily but politely Carole disengages herself. She has learned to recognise when further argument is fruitless, better invest her energies in something productive which will help a starving child, a grieving widow, a father who has lost everything.

Why can't people understand, she thinks to herself. I'm not interested in the power plays or the politics. My only interest in military equipment is my flak-jacket.

To me it's a war of people. The pawns sacrificed to the kings, queens and knights. It is the way it has been for millennia on the banks of the Nile, in the Valley of the Tiber, west of the Shannon.

To hell or to Connacht was the cry in Ireland, but Bosnians do not have a Connacht. No safe haven where they can settle once more and try to live with some dignity. Always, there will be someone who does not like their creed, their customs or the colour of their faces.

But these are not the only criticisms which Carole receives and she sometimes wonders how people can be so callous in their comments. Do they not realise she has feelings too? Do they think she does not care about her family? Do they not know that it is rude to approach someone and say it would be far better if you stayed at home with your family, than chasing over and back to Bosnia.

Of course she would prefer to be sitting at home by the fireside, sipping coffee, looking at Glenroe and helping Kristian with one of his puzzles than being in some draughty warehouse sorting clothes into sizes, sexes and ages.

Would she not prefer to be listening to stories of school from Sarah than bending her ear in a noisy dance-hall to hear a suggested solution to the Bosnian conflict.

Naturally she would prefer watching Audrey on stage in Carrigaline than listening to a rock group a hundred miles away in the small hours of the morning.

And what kind of choice is there between helping Mark with homework in the safety of her living room to dodging through the back streets of Mostar hampered by a flak-jacket which is of dubious value anyway, as she delivers supplies to a kindly doctor who hasn't been paid for over a year.

If she doesn't do these things, who will? No one is canvassing for her particular job right now. It is so easy to criticise from the sidelines, the ditch is such a comfortable seat for hurlers. She is sometimes saddened by what her children have missed, but they understand why and have grown through the experience.

They have a good father, grandparents and other family, when so many in Bosnia have no one. She often remembers the ten year old she met on one visit who had spent two weeks living in a cave because all his family were dead and he was afraid the soldiers would come back. Who could deny him help? Carole is often haunted by the face of the little girl Sabrina who looked at her so plaintively with impossibly brown eyes from a hospital bed in Mostar. She had extensive stomach wounds from a shrapnel burst and had her hands strapped to the bed to prevent her itching the healing wounds. What was her future? Is she still alive? Was she just cured of her injuries to be sent out to die in the next Mortar attack? Did she end up in a rape camp?

On the bad nights when Carole wakes at the end of a nightmare it is the face of Sabrina she sees and knows that whatever she does, it will still not be enough. The people who give to the cause know their priorities too and do not stint in their giving.

Occasionally in the past, though it was a rarity in her case, there were letters and articles querying the use of the funds which were donated. While Carole realises that there are many groups and individuals who are channelling aid to Bosnia she knows in her heart there will be someone to abuse it.

All she can do is keep her own operation clean, open to scrutiny and be above board in all her dealings. She takes control of the aid on the Irish side and she is lucky to have someone of the calibre of Áine to receive it on the other side. When she can, she goes out herself to help her colleague with the work but if she never got out she would be confident of their route and distribution.

Someone makes in every war, there would be no war otherwise, and it would surprise Carole if there weren't people profiting from this war too. Even in Ireland during the "Emergency", fortunes were made on the black market. Tea surfaced in the most unlikely places, and tobacco became almost a currency of it's own. The conflict in Northern Ireland is also fuelled by greed and extortion and there is no trouble spot in the world where money does not play an active role.

So too in Bosnia there are those who are prepared to shamelessly exploit the misery of others. If they are prepared to kill people, what's so wrong with taking their money.

But to concentrate on that would be a reason to stop, she could not do that and live with herself later. She thinks of Audrey who sometime before had been asked why her mother was always collecting for Bosnia.

"She says she couldn't look at herself in the mirror if she didn't" was her reply, which brought peals of laughter from the adult company she was in just then. But it was true. They need it, I can do it, is Carole's creed and the critics, cynics and sideline experts can keep their counsel to themselves.

12

CONFLICT ROOTED IN HISTORY

Very often the causes and historical reasons for wars are relatively easy to understand and the differences which caused the conflicts quite clear.

Such is not the case with the conflict which now rages in the land which was formerly known as Yugoslavia and it is necessary to delve deep into history for the first inkling of how the present dissent came about.

Whether you go back 600 years to the battle of Kosovo, more recently the opening shot of the First World War in Sarajevo or the choice of different sides by the various ethnic groups in the Hitler inspired Second World War, the answer is rooted in the same diversity of religions, cultures, languages and customs.

There is a useful mnemonic often quoted in diplomatic circles which says that Yugoslavia is one land with two alphabets, three religions, four languages, five main nationalities and six republics.

While it may be simplistic it does show the diversity of the culture of the peoples who make up the former Yugoslavia.

The Serbs traditionally used the Cyrillic alphabet while the Croats adopted the Roman style. Religions comprise the Roman Catholic most widely practised by the Croats and Slovenes, while the Slavic Serbs pursued Eastern orthodoxy and the Bosnian Muslims were loyal to Islam.

Languages comprise Serbo-Croat, Macedonian, Slovene and Croatian. The five nationalities are in order of size, Serbs 40%, Croats 22%, Muslims 8.5%, Slovenes 8% and Macedonians 6%.

The six republics which formed Tito's Yugoslavia were, Bosnia/Hercegovina, Croatia, Macedonia, Montenegro, Serbia and Slovenia.

As far back as the 14th Century the Danube formed the border between the Austro/Hungarian Empire of the west and the Turkish Empire of the East.

The territories of Slovenia and Croatia were traditionally western influenced even as far back as the 8th century and in latter time Slovenia was the only Yugoslav Republic to share a border with a Western European Country.

With subsequent conquests of various parts of the Balkan lands, different areas with a variety of ethnic groups were conquered and taken over by various European and Eastern powers.

Thus the Serbs lost lands to the Croats, and vice versa with artificial majorities being created in different regions. Dalmatia for instance, with a good percentage of both populations fell to Austria in 1797 after the Napoleonic campaign in Italy and continued under its control until the empire finally ceased to exist in 1918.

On 1st December of that year the Kingdom of the Serbs, Croats and Slovenes was set up under a Serbian monarchy. Part of that territory had been promised to Italy after the war if they supported the allies, but lost their claim on the establishment of the kingdom.

However, in the years following, the Croats and Slovenes became unhappy with Serb dominance and in 1929 the Kingdom of Yugoslavia was set up with Government by royal dictatorship.

After World War II the differences expressed amongst the various ethnic groups were firmly suppressed by the emerging dictator Josip Broz Tito who was to continue to govern Yugoslavia until his death on 4th May 1980.

He ruled his country with an iron fist, but managed to mould the six republics and two Autonomous Provinces in Serbia into one united state.

He quickly and ruthlessly suppressed any ethnic calls for recognition, but did apply equal treatment to all constituent republics.

Though originally aligned with the U.S.S.R., he quickly tired of their attentions and in 1948 declared Yugoslavia to be a non-aligned state. In subsequent years he found himself in the company of other countries who were strange allies, but he never faltered from his course.

In common with most of Europe, Yugoslavia had been occupied by the Germans during the Second World War. The occupation was resisted by the Cetniks, a group comprising former members of the Army, and the Partisans, a communist led force.

The population of Yugoslavia was always tough and it is interesting to note that it was the only country to gain its freedom in the Second World War without Allied help. The resistance movement managed to tie up as many German divisions as Rommel had available to him in North Africa

The Serbians in particular had suffered greatly under German domination while the Croatians chose not to oppose them.

It was through the Partisans that Tito derived his power and on the fall of the German administration stepped into the vacuum.

While he ruled in a harsh and repressive manner, he did have the good of Yugoslavia at heart. He set up the Rotating Collective Federal Presidency in which each of the eight constituent Republics and Provinces had the right to nominate a member. The presidency of this collective rotated, with each constituent region providing the incumbent in turn.

Tito also gave the two enclaves within Serbia, Kosovo with a majority of Albanians and Vojvodina which was home to the Hungarians of Serbia, total autonomy which was recognised as a far-sighted and wise decision. In the constitution of 1974 they were given the status of republics.

But on his death in 1980 it was widely expected that the problems and unrest which had been suppressed during his regime would once more re-emerge.

His system of Government was to prove unworkable without his dominating force and it was to be only a matter of time before the country would start to break up.

The Soviet President, Leonid Brezhnev had said that when forces hostile to socialism seek to reverse the development of any socialist country whatsoever, this becomes the concern of all socialist countries.

It was this principle enunciated and supported by the Soviet Union as much as any other factor which kept Yugoslavia together in the years immediately after Tito's death.

But Brezhnev could hardly have foreseen the fall of Communism in the decade after his death and was not to know how much it would be facilitated by his eventual successor Mikhail Gorbachev.

Against a background of a resurgence of Nationalism in Eastern Europe Gorbachev told the world from the Helsinki Conference of 25th October 1989 that the doctrine enunciated by Brezhnev was buried.

This was to give the final go-ahead for the democratisation of many of the European Soviet Satellites and to a great extent the emasculation of the communist parties of many of those countries.

All over Europe the lights of freedom and democracy which had been extinguished by Hitler and Stalin were once more beginning to come back on, and there was hope that the subjugated peoples would again find the freedom they so desperately longed for.

Who could have thought that the fall of communism could have come so swiftly. In 1989 when the various communist regions loosened their stranglehold the people took the initiative gratefully.

In February, Hungary led the way, followed by Poland in June. In November, Bulgaria, East Germany and Czechoslovakia snapped their chains and in December Romania finally ousted Ceaucescu.

Albania, the last of the Soviet Republics fell in 1990 and most significant of all, East Germany ceased to exist on 3rd October. By January of 1992 every Eastern European country had freely and fairly elected governments. Significantly all were non-communist, though in Romania and Albania ex-communists retained much of the power.

In 1990 Yugoslavia too renounced Communism, which was openly predicted in Slovenia as far back as 1988. The press had become far more daring, criticising government, the socialist system and Soviet control.

If however freedoms were growing in some parts of Yugoslavia, Serbian President Slobodan Milosevic had designs on other areas of the country which might be brought under Serbian control.

Within its borders the republics of Kosovo and Vojvodina with majorities of Albanians and Hungarians were hoping for greater freedom. However Milosevic pushed through constitutional changes which strengthened effective Serbian control over their territories and any hopes of independence they might have had, began to dim.

In Moscow, Mikhail Gorbachev was pre-occupied with his own difficulties in trying to turn around the economy, and even if the dissatisfaction in the satellites was noticed it drew little or no reaction.

With the ending of the Cold War, Yugoslavia was becoming less and less important as a buffer between the superpowers and merited less attention from West and East as the decades-old tensions eased. This was to become particularly evident as the situation in Croatia and subsequently Bosnia/Hercegovina steadily disimproved and when all out war started neither side wanted to know.

By 1990 Croatian leaders were talking openly about independence and the break up of Yugoslavia, which had been forecast, was becoming more and more a reality.

That year all six republics held the first free elections since 1938. Croatia elected a non Communist government with Franjo Tudjman as President after his party won 200 of the 356 seats.

Tudjman guaranteed ethnic, cultural and all other rights to all citizens and said what he wanted most of all was a Parliamentary Democracy. They were more than aware from the experience of other countries just what lay ahead if they wanted to make economic progress.

In Slovenia also, Nationalist Democrats won decisively but former Communists won in Serbia. The seeds of the conflict which was to follow were beginning to germinate.

Serbia, seeing the other Republics begin the transition to separate statehood, began to prepare itself to pursue the goal of a greater Serbia. Pushed into conflict by the right wing Cetniks, it looked for the transfer of parts of Macedonia, Montenegro, Bosnia/Hercegovina and Croatia as well as the Republics of Kosovo and Vojvodina which were contained entirely within their borders.

By December 1990 a full scale Civil War was predicted by the C.I.A. but still the west was reluctant to get involved to help the birth of the emerging nations.

In September of 1989 Slovenia had declared her right to secede from the Federation and held a referendum on Independence on 23rd December 1990. This was overwhelmingly carried and the first cracks began to appear on the veneer of Yugoslavia unity.

With Communism and Tito gone, decades old restraints went as well. Communism had kept the Eastern European peoples from achieving the social compromises and accommodations worked out in Western countries. These would now be worked out with weapons rather than diplomacy.

Despite threats from the Federal Communist Party, and disenchanted at the slow pace of reform, Slovenia on 20th

February 1991 voted for constitutional change which would allow for a greater element of self-determination while still staying within the Federation.

Slovenia with a population of 2 million people, 90% of whom are Slovenes always had a western outlook and was physically the closest of the Yugoslav republics to western influence.

They had good productivity, a buoyant economy and at one point in the 1970's were importing labour to keep their factories going.

Some of the 169,000 strong Federal Army dominated by Serbs was sent to Slovenia to maintain its borders. With a population of just 2% Serbs, and Slovenia having no apparent designs on expanding its borders, the Serbs saw no need to interfere militarily.

It appeared Slovenia had got away with it's daring. They looked to the west for support, but got little satisfaction from E.C. Commission President Jacques Delors, who saw in disintegrating Yugoslavia, the opposite of the unity he wished to achieve in Europe, despite the fact that several of the new Republics would more than likely apply for membership of the E.C. sooner or later.

In 1991 the rotating collective presidency was held by Serbia's Borisav Jovic who it was felt was unduly influenced by Serbian President Milosevic, only partly balanced by the Croatian Federal Prime Minister Ante Markovic.

By March tensions were high and it was clear that the country was gearing up to conflict ahead.

The Republics publicly flexed their muscles as they prepared either to defend what they had or extend their area of influence by military means.

Serbia was already talking of linking all the lands in which Serbs lived regardless of the Republic to which it belonged. At the same time Croatia was talking of restoring Croatia's natural borders where Croats would be in a majority.

Bosnia/Hercegovina would be one of the republics which would attract the attentions of its neighbours and here the Bosnian Muslims had most to lose.

All it would take was for the Serbian dominated Federal Government to send in the Serbian dominated Yugoslav National Army to "protect" Serbian minorities and the country would be in turmoil.

For the moment they resisted but an armed uprising threatened in Kosovo, that could provide the spark which would set flame to the tinder-dry political scene.

In May Serbia and Montenegro refused to ratify the appointment of the incoming Croatian nominee for the Federal Presidency, something which under the decades-old arrangement should have been automatic. This was in retaliation for Croatia's move towards independence, not appreciated by the like-minded Republics of Serbia and Montenegro.

On 26th June 1991 Slovenia and Croatia made the inevitable declaration of independence but predictably the federal government refused to recognise the states. Instead the Federal Army moved in to restore the status-quo.

Slovenia was considered of little strategic importance to Serbia, counting only 2% Serbs among its 2 million population. A cease-fire was arranged and the country was left largely in peace.

In December along with other republics Slovenia requested world recognition. Germany was first to declare for the new sovereign state on 23rd December and was followed by the EC in January 1992.

Meanwhile in Croatia the fighting was fierce. Within a month of it's June 1991 declaration heavy casualties were being reported and by August the massacres had begun.

Reports of the first major war crimes came from the Croatian town of Vukovar where in late August it is estimated that up to 7,000 people died in nine hours. The Serb shelling was intense and directed as much at the civilian population as the military.

When the shelling stopped, the soldiers moved in killing, maiming and torturing those they met. Evidence of the atrocities is horrific and later returning refugees were met with a catalogue of devastation and death not seen in Europe since 1945. These were the foundation for retaliatory attacks later on.

This immediately hardened attitudes and the country settled down to a war of attrition. Croatia is home to a large minority of Serbs (11.5%) and the areas in which they lived became a target for Serbian expansionism.

By September Croatia had lost one-third of its territory to the Serbs, who as well as the Yugoslav National Army had the backing of the irregular Cetnik force.

In October Slovenia and Croatia began implementing their sovereignty declarations and withdrew from the collective Presidency. The balance of the Presidency consisting of Serbia, Montenegro, Kosovo and Vojvodina continued in power.

Bosnia/Hercegovina declared its sovereignty in mid October and the die was cast.

Even before the military conflict was a couple of months old, Irish Times Contributor Petar Hadji-Ristic wrote on 6th July 1991 :-

"Cry not the end of Yugoslavia, some say, but what is unfolding is a tragedy of untold dimensions" he wrote. "It is a story of a regime - personified now by the army and the Serbian leader, Slobodan Milosevic - so depraved and corrupt that it has proved incapable of peaceful reform.

What could have been the first country to break with communism in Europe had ended up the last in line, with possibly the most violent consequences.

But Yugoslavia was doomed, some insist by the diversity of its people, its different religions, languages and so on.

There was so much toing and froing between its republics, marriages between its peoples and friendships across today's battle lines, such a mix of nations within republics that this cannot be the case; it was only doomed, if it is, by the poverty of vision of its dogmatic leadership.

One need only look as far as the declared determination of the rebels of Slovenia and Croatia to aim for membership of another community of nations - the European Community - to see they are ready to live with others".

And in the midst of this was Bosnia/Hercegovina a target for the attentions of both Serbia and Croatia and which had traditionally been a buffer between them.

Traditional enmity had been again revived by political alignments during the Second World War. The Croatian Ustase and Serbian Cetniks, two irregular forces, had fought with the Germans in that conflict while the Serb Partisans had maintained the resistance to occupation.

Memories of Serbian and Croatian excesses during the war were revived and in one particularly clumsy and offensive incident, the skeletons of Serbs killed in the war were dug up in the full glare of media attention on the instructions of the Serb leadership.

The idea clearly was to rekindle old hatreds and to some extent must have been successful.

On 3rd March 1992 Bosnia/Hercegovina following a referendum in the previous days declared its independence, an act which was guaranteed to draw military reaction from the now totally Serb dominated Federal Government and Army.

President of the new State was Alija Izetbegovic, the leader of the Muslim Party of Democratic Action, fully supported by the Croat population in Bosnia/Hercegovina.

The Bosnian Serbs had boycotted the referendum and opposed independence and on March 27th declared the Serbian Republic of Bosnia/Hercegovina under the leadership of the Serbian Democratic Party, Radovan Karadzic. This was the final trigger for full civil war, the ferocity of which could not have been anticipated even by the most pessimistic observers.

This was a three party war and initially the Croatians linked with the Muslims against the common enemy Serbia. But if Karadzic and Milosevic had any diplomatic or military expertise it was in the area of divide and conquer. Without this tactic it would be a long bitter contest without the prospect of success.

By May 1992 the full horror of the war in Bosnia/Hercegovina was becoming known and if the world thought the Croatian fight for freedom was bloody they had far worse to come.

In March Bosnian Serbs had declared an autonomous "Serbian Republic of Bosnia/Hercegovina" with its capital in Banja Luka and on 12th May decided to form its own Government and armed forces.

Later in July the Bosnian Croats under Mate Boban proclaimed the "Croatian Community of Herceg - Bosna" in these areas of Bosnia controlled by Croat forces.

It moved Martin Bell of the B.B.C. writing in The Spectator on 23rd May 1992 to comment on the one and only peace march held on the night of the Referendum for Independence and the happenings in the weeks afterwards.

"Some seven weeks later" he wrote "we are deep into the most uncontrolled blood-letting in Europe since the Second World War. At one point I counted 17 different battlefields - as certainly an underestimate as the latest total of dead, some 1,300. The killing rate is roughly ten times what it was at the equivalent stage of the war for Croatia. It is a war in which civilians - including Red Cross workers - are not only not spared, but targeted with peculiar ferocity: routinely tortured before death and mutilated afterwards. The plight of refugees - the numbers conservatively put at half a million is again the greatest in Europe since the war. This forced migration of peoples is not just the consequence but, in many cases, the intended effect of the fighting".

He said it was hard to explain why the model for tolerance in Yugoslavia should have fallen into chaos and why Sarajevo which survived two world wars virtually intact "should now be a smoking ruin, neither its mosques nor churches spared".

"Part of the answer has to lie in leadership, or lack of it: a willingness to play on the old fears and hatreds. Part lies in

military and political incoherence, in which neither side controls its own gunmen and every roadblock has its own Napoleon. Part of it lies in outside intervention, especially by Serbian paramilitary and the government in Belgrade, aggressively intent on protecting their own even where their own are not directly threatened; but also by the Croats - again on the argument of defending their own - funnelling at least four brigades of main force units across the border so that Zagreb's writ may also run in Hercegovina.

"Yet the Serbs already control more than 64% of Bosnia" he wrote later. "They have confined their enemies to the beleaguered pockets of Moslem and Croatian strength. They are poised to seize the capital or its ruins. They have reduced the legally elected Government of Bosnia to a point where it hardly controls the streets outside the Presidency. And the Serbian war machine rolls on, daily strengthened by men and munitions from the dissolving garrisons of the Yugoslav National Army: Where will it end".

Almost two years on, there still seems to be no end. The city of Sarajevo which Karadzic said in May 1991 he could take anytime is still under siege with horrific conditions imposed on the inhabitants.

By July of 1992 there was no respite in sight and Europe was faced with its worst refugee problem in fifty years. But the capitals of Europe did not accept the responsibility and left the leadership of the warring factions to sort out the human problems.

More content with making war, or unable because of the war to deal with civilian casualties, the inhabitants of Croatia and Bosnia/Hercegovina caught in the war zone suffered alone.

The only ones to hear their pleas for help were the official aid agencies and voluntary workers who started their long campaign on behalf of first, the people of Croatia and later the people of Bosnia/Hercegovina.

By now as Martin Bell had perceived, the government of Bosnia/Hercegovina had lost control of most of the territory which it had at the time of the declaration of independence.

It had little in the way of a domestic arms industry and with the U.N. imposed arms embargo found itself in very poor circumstances militarily. By contrast the Serbian forces originally supplied by the Yugoslav National Army had access to the limitless supplies which had been reportedly topped up substantially from the Eastern Bloc prior to the outbreak of hostilities. The Bosnian Croats continued to be supplied by Croatia which also helped in some measure to supply the Muslims of Bosnia/Hercegovina with arms. Muslim aid also arrived from some of the Islamic countries of the East.

With the take-over of territories came the practice of ethnic cleansing, something which was brought to a fine art during the summer of 1992 by the victorious Serbian forces. This consisted of captured areas being systematically stripped of its ethnic population through the killing, ill-treatment, bullying and expulsion of civilians.

Stories of civil rights violations emerged by the thousand and later, a shocked world population would hear about the rape camps, a particularly heinous form of torture directed mainly at Croatian and Muslim women.

The U.N. would start to investigate such reports as well as massacres but would be hampered in their efforts by the war.

On the military side, the World's Police Organisation sent in a force of 21,000 troops to Bosnia/Hercegovina under Canadian command, but their mandate amounted only to the protection of humanitarian aid convoys.

By the end of 1992, thirty of their number had been killed and 300 wounded.

In January the U.N. had prepared a peace plan for the area and Lord Carrington had been brought in to broker a peace settlement for Bosnia/Hercegovina. This was a failure as were all the U.N. attempts largely due to the intractability of the

Serbs, who, as the force which was making the most ground strove to abide by the first rule of war "what you have you hold".

In all nine cease-fires were negotiated by the E.C. and the U.N. all of which proved fruitless.

Lord Carrington's special envoy in Sarajevo was Colm Doyle who in the words of Martin Bell of the B.B.C. had spent weeks negotiating cease-fires against the odds and had gained a reputation for fair dealing even among the Serbs.

"Mr. Doyle", wrote Bell "is a professional soldier and about as ambiguous as a blunderbuss - but in Bosnia a most effective diplomat. (One can only envy the Irish Army, such must be the wealth of talent in its upper echelons that in his other life he is but a humble Major, and Commander of small-town garrisons).

The point about Mr. Doyle is not that he failed but that he tried - and that, in trying, he certainly saved some lives."

Sanctions had been imposed on Yugoslavia by the E.C. and the United States though they were only continued in Serbia and Montenegro after the other republics had implemented their independence declarations.

The war ground its way inexorably on through the first half of 1993 taking a terrible toll on the population through the long winter.

Countless numbers died in the fighting, countless more through hunger and the intense cold. Temperatures of minus 20°C are a regular feature of the Balkan region and in their makeshift shelters the people died through lack of heat, anything approaching a balanced diet and the battle for land, prestige and power which raged around them.

By the Spring, the full horrors began to emerge and with the milder weather and drier underfoot conditions, the armies were better able to wage their campaigns. This had long ceased to be, if indeed it ever had been, a war between military forces.

Sarajevo continued to withstand the siege and was typical of what was happening all over Bosnia/Hercegovina. This city of almost half a million people was founded in its present form by the Turks in 1435. Several of the buildings of that time had been preserved though it is unlikely that anything of interest and particularly buildings of Turkish architecture will survive the present war. It is a beautiful city nestling among the hills, though they have become notorious for sheltering the Serb gunners who daily pound the town. The city gained an everlasting place in the history books on 28th July 1914 when Gavrilo Princip assassinated the heir to the Austro/Hungarian Empire, Ferdinand and his wife Sophia thus precipitating the First World War. Now, food supplies were virtually nil coming into the city, with humanitarian aid coming into the airport when it could be maintained open.

People lived in shelters as they tried to avoid the bombardment at night. By day they scurried along the streets always fearful of the snipers bullet, the mortar lobbed carelessly from the hills or directed with cynical precision at a bread queue, a hospital queue or line of people at one of the few water taps working in the city.

Deliberately targeted too were hospitals, schools and churches, places of refuge traditionally respected but in this war - as Martin Bell reported about Red Cross Workers - made the deliberate targets of Serbian aggression.

Daily the death toll mounted, the world watched and spoke of brave Sarajevo but did little else.

All over Bosnia/Hercegovina, communities with Muslim/Croatian populations came under siege and towns whose names had heretofore not been known outside of Eastern Europe suddenly were on the lips of the worlds population.

Towns like Gorazde where the suffering was unspeakable the splendid port city of Dubrovnik whose distinct medieval architecture was destroyed in weeks, in an orgy of bombardment.

Another victim was Banja Luka in the heart of Serb territory in Bosnia which in March would become the Capital of what was styled the "Serbian Republic of Bosnia/Hercegovina". Within a short time, all fifteen mosques and many of the churches in the city had been levelled in an orgy of destruction by the Serbs.

Tuzla in the mountains of northern Bosnia would also pay a heavy price as the Serbs strove for their greater Serbia, oblivious to the hardships they were inflicting and the hatreds they were creating which would last for generations. Names like Zepa, Mostar and Bosanski Brod became all too familiar.

Radovan Karadzic, the former psychiatrist was inflicting more than a huge psychological toll on the inhabitants of "his" country and was oblivious to the pleas which came from within and without Bosnia/Hercegovina for an end to the mad campaign.

By mid-year, "The Bosnia/Hercegovina of the democratically elected Alija Izetbegovic" had virtually ceased to exist and the pall of smoke from the barrels of so many guns, and the burning of homes which hung over the country was matched only by the stench of death which arose from street, field and mountainside.

Roads were jammed with refugees who were dispossessed and who fled their homes lucky to be alive, victims of a campaign, harmlessly described in the antiseptic phrase "ethnic cleansing".

The U.N. had not provided the mandate, the manpower nor the firepower to protect the communities. The world wrung its hands in horror and as it saw the Muslim and Croatian population mown down, it withheld the necessary arms from them with which they might have defended themselves.

Victims of the western embargo on the sale of arms to the region, the Croats and Muslims were denied the capacity to fight back "lest it escalate the violence in the region".

A corridor from Split to Sarajevo was contemplated to ensure a continuance of food supplies but it was estimated that because of the terrain it would require a force the size of the British Army to maintain it.

Even protecting convoys and getting them through perimeter forces seemed a major task for the U.N. and they operated mainly as an ineffective force, underarmed, under equipped and often reduced, at least in the eyes of the local population, to the role of chauffeur for the leaders of the various factions going to and from cease-fire talks.

The men on the ground tried but got little support from the constituent nations of the U.N. Peace plans came and went and the Carrington talks ended in failure.

In September 1992 former U.S. Secretary of State Cyrus Vance and Britain's Lord David Owen co-chaired a peace conference in Geneva which was to produce a blueprint for peace in the region.

Immediately Bosnian Serb leader Karadzic proposed a three way division of Bosnia/Hercegovina which did not take account of the majority position of the Muslims of the area who accounted for 44% of the population.

If there had been any doubt about the intentions of the Serb war-machine and the purpose of the territorial gains in both Croatia and Bosnia/Hercegovina they were dispelled with the format of the first map produced for the future of the region.

There was hope that the newly elected American President Bill Clinton would want to stamp his authority on the world order. If not that, at least humanitarian considerations might inspire him to action. Without an American lead it was unlikely the U.N. would take any action which would require major military support.

By January of 1993 the intention was to carve Bosnia/Hercegovina into ten ethnic provinces and this was accepted by all sides, though very reluctantly by Karadzic. While the principle might have been agreed though, the drawing of the map would cause real difficulties.

It had been an expensive year for Bosnia in human terms, with over 150,000 dead, virtually all of whom were civilians, and 800,000 homeless people. 2.3 million people had been moved in an operation designed to "re-balance" certain ethnic areas.They were not to know it then, but many must have suspected the inevitable, that the following year would be little better for the people.

Croatia had had enjoyed relative stability within its borders having allowed a U.N. force to deploy in the Serb dominated region of Krajina in April. They had lost 7,500 dead, one sixth of them soldiers with almost 25,000 injured.

Bosnia/Hercegovina had been divided into three if not geographically or politically, at least ethnically. It was difficult to see what more the Muslims could lose, but the Serbs were not yet ready to concede, not having achieved their full military goals and with still more territorial gains possible.

Their foothold on the Adriatic was precarious and would need to be expanded, and there was more land to be won from both the Croats and Muslims of Bosnia/Hercegovina.

With the dawn of 1993 it was difficult to imagine any further horrors which could befall the tormented people of Bosnia/Hercegovina. We had seen the bodies of soldiers in their defence lines, the massacred civilians in the streets and the gaunt faces of the internees in the Serb concentration camps.

They looked through the wire with the same hopelessness and hollow-eyed despair, the same emaciated bodies with which we had seen the Jews of the Second World War look on the uncaring world. The West knew but chose inaction.

What new horrors could come from this land whose population had long since been shocked into the numbness of despair. But still some hoped that the west would act, would come to their assistance. An Amnesty International advertisement in November 1992 showed a photograph of a line of shaven-headed men in a Serbian concentration camp with the headline "Take a good look. Don't ever say I didn't know it was happening".

The text goes on to say "Orla Guerin, R.T.E.'s Eastern Europe correspondant, tells us that when she was leaving Sarajevo recently a young Muslim with tears streaming down his face pleaded with her saying; "Please tell the world what is happening".

She says "I didn't have the heart to tell him that the world already knows".

Reports began to emerge of a new weapon aimed primarily at the Muslim women of Bosnia. The world was to hear about the Rape Camps which were to serve the Serbian war machine as effectively as their army.

If their only purpose was for the enjoyment of the troops returning from the front the world might have had some understanding if not acceptance. Women have always ranked high in the spoils of war.

But the Serbian intention ran much deeper than that. It was a plan designed to upset the whole fabric of society in Muslim Bosnia. A raped Muslim woman no longer has a place in her home, her village, her society. She is ostracised.

The husband of a Muslim woman so treated will not stay in his town or village. He will leave, thus contributing, at least unwittingly to the Serbian policy of ethnic cleansing.

With the election of Bill Clinton to the White House and his official arrival there in January 1993, the watching world expected some firm action on the war in Bosnia. Having campaigned on the promise of tougher action against Serbia, that watching world was disappointed, as Clinton, increasingly caught up with domestic policy and hearing forecasts of "another Vietnam", shelved any thoughts of military intervention.

In March as reports began to emerge of people eating their dead to survive in Eastern Bosnia, a plan to airlift food to the beleaguered towns was conceived by the U.S. It was a stop-gap measure at best, in some respects a cosmetic exercise only, and fraught with difficulties in its execution.

Dropping supplies from 10,000 feet instead of the usual 400 in order to avoid anti-aircraft fire made the operation hap-hazard in the extreme and the difficulties of the recipients were no less.

People could be hit and killed by the falling pallets, gathering the supplies in daylight would make them targets for snipers and the arrival of much needed supplies among a starving population could cause its own local dissent.

Srebrenica was a name with which the world became all too familiar. A town of 60,000 people it had for some months been attracting the military attentions of Serbia. Located in Eastern Bosnia it was one of a series of towns in the region of that country which bordered on Serbia and which made it an obvious area into which Serbia could expand.

One by one the towns came under siege and every tactic was employed to make life unbearable for the local, predominantly Muslim, population.

Tuzla, Cerska and Srebrenica became names synonymous with Muslim suffering and Serbian aggression but still the west did not respond in any meaningful way.

"In the name of God do something" they heard the amateur radio operator call from Srebrenica but after one year of ethnic cleansing the Serbs knew the west was not committed to any military intervention. They had a free hand and used it very effectively.

There was talk of air-strikes against Serbian artillery in the hills which daily bombarded the besieged towns. There was even talk of deploying ground troops, but threats that Serbia would take the war to London and Washington broke any Western resolve there might have been.

It was left to General Philippe Morillon to salvage some pride for his country, the U.N. and their soldiers on the ground. In March in a memorable stand-off with the Serbs he broke through to Srebrenica and to the delight of the Muslim population stood solidly with them there. He is reported to have witnessed them eating their dead and he stood by them until aid was eventually allowed through. Later, the Bosnian Envoy to the U.N. withdrew and apologised for these reports which he said were false, though Carole still feels that the retraction may have been forced upon him.

This does not take from Morrillon's achievements, and at last people could see initiative on the ground. So proud were people of the decisiveness and moral steel that Morillon and his men had shown that he earned the title Beau Geste internationally and in Bosnia "General Courage".

For once, the Serbs had been faced down, but the lesson wasn't learned and the west once more settled into its lethargy and relied on an increasingly fruitless Vance/Owen initiative to mollify public concern.

The best the U.N. in New York could do was declare Srebrenica a safe-haven for Muslims. Despite public indignation and outcry the governments of the U.N. countries, most involved continued to stand back and not only did they fail to protect the largely undefended Muslim population they refused to lift the embargo on arms shipments to the least well armed of the three protagonists even for defensive purposes.

The Muslims could not have been viewed as an offensive force even if they had tried to recover some of their land from Serbia whose campaign had increased their area of influence to 70% of Bosnian territory. Historians in the future will wonder where the Bosnian Muslims co-religionists of the Middle East were, in their time of need. Would an offer of military help from that quarter have galvanised the west to action or would their intervention have triggered a full-scale international conflict.

So many signals were sent to Serbian President Slobodan Milosevic and his partner in war-crime, the Bosnian Serb leader Radovan Karadzic that the west was militarily paralysed and diplomatically frozen, that they felt free to do what they liked.

They had defied the U.N., broken cease-fires at will, signed a peace-plan they did not intend to keep, all without retaliation from the west. They and their generals had effective carte blanche and they would use it effectively.

In the full glare of Western publicity, Srebrenica and Tuzla succumbed and the U.N. in their evacuation plan were forced to carry out the ethnic cleansing for the Serbs. They in their turn were content to see the U.N. carry out what for them would be a time-consuming operation. The Serbs were always winners.

The Vance/Owen plan for 10 ethnic regions was in ruins. Srebrenica was to have been for the Muslims and that could not be enforced. Mostar was given to Croatia and they moved quickly to consolidate their gains. The 43% of Bosnia assigned to the Serbs under the plan had been militarily increased to 70% and while there were plums there for the picking, Serbia was more than ready to attend to the harvest.

Through the Summer the map was drawn and redrawn at the request of Alija Izetbegovic but each time the territory the Muslims were allocated seemed to get smaller as the Serbs continued to expand their area of domination. There was no rush on Serbia to settle and the Muslims were almost on their knees. Except for a few safe havens, guaranteed at a distance by the U.N. their writ did not run in Bosnia and all that was left was for Serbia and Croatia to agree between them on the carve-up of this unfortunate country.

In a year and a half, the Muslim community had been reduced from a reasonable lifestyle to the battered remnants of a distinct nation. What shot and shell had not achieved had been finished by weather, hunger and disease.

The Owen proposal of early August 1993 that Bosnia should be divided three ways with the Muslims receiving 30% seemed hollow, as they then occupied only 10% of the region. Without acceptance by Serbia or a determined effort by the west to enforce it, the plan had little hope of success.

It was a complicated settlement with a requirement on the U.N. to maintain corridors between ethnic regions, the E.C. to administer Mostar and an undertaking from the Serbs to cease aggression.

It was a plan seen by the Muslims as a reward for aggression. Their territory was in three distinct areas and any prospect of a unitary homeland would be dashed for all time. Even Lord Owen conceded it was not a fair plan, but with no one ready to commit ground combat troops, that was the best on offer.

Through the Winter of 1993/94, the war ground inexorably on with media attention concentrating mainly on Sarajevo. The siege there had now been in place for a year and a half and there was no show of force to try to break it.

Christmas came and went with occasional cease-fires which rarely held more than a few hours or a day at most. The fighting between Croats and Muslims grew fiercer much to the delight of the Serbs and conditions in Mostar grew steadily worse as fewer and fewer humanitarian aid trucks got through.

The turning point in the war came on Saturday 5th February when a Mortar bomb landed in a busy market in Sarajevo killing 69 people and injuring hundreds of others. This was the last straw and the U.N. at last began to take action. Though it was not officially established, all evidence pointed to the atrocity being instigated by Serb forces.

Prompted by their Commander in Bosnia, Britain's General Rose, the U.N. issued an ultimatum to the Serbs to withdraw their artillery to a point twenty miles from Sarajevo and gave a deadline for this to be carried out or risk air-strikes by U.N. planes.

The Serbs held out to the last minute claiming weather conditions prevented them completing the task but it was just a face-saving exercise. They had done enough to satisfy the United Nations who for the first time since General Morrillon's stay in Srebrenica had shown their teeth.

A week later Serbian military aircraft defied the U.N. ban and bombed a Muslim munitions factory. Four of the planes were shot down as they returned to base and the point was again made to the Serbian military command and political leaders.

For once the Serbs had been faced down, the cease-fire in Sarajevo held and there was talk of that strategy being extended to other areas of the country.

Could this be the beginning of the end? Was the two year agony of Bosnia/Hercegovina about to draw to a close. Only time and U.N. commitment would tell, but with more blue helmets being sent to Bosnia then there was some chance. What seemed an explosive international situation in February might have turned to a damp squib.

On Friday the 18th of March Bosnia and Croatia signed a peace-pact which promised to end the hostilities between them. All that was left was for the Serbs to take a meaningful role in the peace process and progress could be made. There were even strong indications that the siege of Sarajevo might soon be lifted, though one learned never to expect anything in Bosnia until it actually happened.

On March 30th, Croatia signed a ceasefire accord with rebel Serbs who had taken over the Krajina region and had triggered the Croatian war in the process. This was further welcome progress, though with renewed heavy fighting in Gorazde it was evident that the war was not finally over.

Perhaps at last though, the end of the Balkan conflict was at least in sight.

13

GARLIC MUSHROOMS AT 3A.M.

Tony has himself mentally prepared for the usual Friday night trip to see the Dixies who have promised to do a series of dances for Carole over the winter. The money is welcome for the fund, and Carole is building up more and more contacts which will translate into much needed food and medical supplies for Mostar and Ulog, the little village which she, Áine Fr. Seán O'Driscoll and Eamonn Timmins had visited high up in the mountains above Mostar.

Tonight will be more demanding than usual with a hundred mile trip to Newcastle West and a stop in Coachford where the Aghabullogue G.A.A. Club will be running a Progressive 45 Drive for the Fund.

They always try to get on the road early which gives them a more relaxed drive and a little time to chat with the organisers before the event.

It's not always easy however, to break away from the demands of the family and Tony and Carole linger with the children a little longer than usual. For them it is Friday night too, and a break from school. They like the easier atmosphere when there are no demands for lessons to be produced and checked, and preparations to be made for school the following day. The house is warm and homely and eventually Carole and Tony have to make a conscious decision to go.

Caroline, their nineteen year old baby-sitter and "Carole's right hand" arrives and assumes control and Kristian and Audrey look for an extension of their bedtime.

It's easy to concede and anyway they will probably get around Caroline easily enough after they have gone.

At 9.30 pm they leave home and hope they can get back before too late. Tony had stayed to catch the forecast which confirmed that the atrocious weather conditions of the previous week will last into the following day. No joy there.

Just outside Carrigaline in the dark and rain, there is a difference of opinion on the route to Coachford. Tony's navigational ability and his natural sense of direction are called into question, but he prevails and is proved right.

It is only twenty miles to Coachford but driving conditions are poor and they reach the village about ten o'clock.

The lines of cars point the way to the hall and they stumble in the door under a shared umbrella which fortunately Tony had remembered to bring. The hall is thick with smoke, loud with voices but much more important, full with people.

Carole is happy for the organisers as she feels badly when a local group has put time and energy, and probably their money, into organising an event from which the people stay away in droves.

That is not be the case tonight. There must be at least sixty tables with six players at each, so success is assured. As they move towards the centre of operations she hears snatches of the inevitable post mortems as the cards are being shuffled.

"You should have come with the King, they knew you had it" and "you should have hit the high man, I only had one trick".

Always when entering a hall or ballroom or hotel which is comfortable, warm and happy, she is reminded of the suffering people in Bosnia where comfort is non-existent. She is pleased to be here, among rural folk who could identify with their brothers and sisters in the villages of Bosnia and she knows that while there are many hardened card-players in the hall there are others who came only to support the cause.

They are made welcome and before they know it there is a cup of tea in front of them. A small army of women is standing by to serve the players during a short interval and they have everything ready and their approach is rehearsed.

Card players do not like to be disturbed so as Carole speaks to them of conditions in Mostar, the tea and barm brack is hastily served from a huge stockpile of buttered slices.

She knows that her attendance alone is enough so Carole contents herself with telling people where their money will go, what it will buy, the lives it will save. She tells them that they have yet to go to Newcastle West and from the corner of her eye she sees one man roll his eyes to heaven as if to say "Have sense woman", or maybe he just wanted to get on with the game.

But sense will have to wait until the war is over. Security for Carole means starvation for someone is distress. Nights out have to be deferred until the killing fields have been cleansed of the blood of the ethnically cleansed. But Coachford has done it's bit. Aghabullogue has not been found wanting and if everyone were as generous, it would be a container a day.

With the applause still ringing across the hall, they once more venture out into the wintry night.

One last consultation together about the wisdom of going on to Newcastle West but they have given their word so they carry on. A glance at the dashboard clock shows 10.40 pm and it's fifty six miles yet to go.

The swish, swish of the wipers keeps the rain at bay but progress is slow, the road is narrow and strange to Tony.

At Dromahane Carole decides to ring home and tell Caroline that they have decided to go on ahead and that she should go to bed rather than stay up for their return. A wise course of action as it turns out.

Shaking the drops from her hair Carole gets back in the car and they estimate how far they have to go. Whether it is only a Cork trait or a countrywide feature, there are few signs for towns outside the county and it will be a long while yet before they see any signs for Newcastle.

Tony reckons that if he can pick up the Dromcollogher road out of Mallow he will be at least heading in the general direction and at Buttevant he sees the first welcome sign for the town Percy Ffrench made famous.

They meet two young girls walking on the road and they stop and give them a lift. They're going towards Broadford, in the pitch black night, and they have no light with them. It's not far off midnight on a dark and terrible night but they ask to be left off at a cross-roads a few miles further on.

Cheerfully they announce as they leave the car that they have only two miles to go and they disappear into the night.

Onwards, ever onwards towards Dromcollogher and Carole remembers that the dance will be finished at midnight. Its' half past as they pass through a deserted Drumcollogher and they decide to keep an eye out for the Dixie's bandwagon.

Twenty minutes later the welcome lights of Newcastle West wink in the distance and Tony asks Carole where the dance is/was.

As often happens, Carole has forgotten what she has been told and they look for someplace with cars outside, that's if the dance is still going on. With relief they are told by a passing pedestrian that the River Room is where they want and they arrive to find that the Dixies are not long on stage.

Sean Lucey and the boys have a smile and a wave for them as they come in and they are relieved to see that the second Bosnia event that night has a good crowd too.

A reporter from the Limerick Leader is waiting for them and whisks Carole away to do an interview. She promises herself she will try and get a copy of the paper but like so many other little personal luxuries, she probably won't.

Later she goes over in her mind her talk to the people. She has learned to gauge the proper length, the appropriate content, the degree of horror she will include. Tonight is not a night for the full story but she does try to convey the sense of loneliness, loss and suffering with which the people of Bosnia have to cope.

185

The crowd is attentive with the exception of a few giggling couples immersed in themselves and oblivious of any hardship there might be outside of the comfortable confines of the River Room.

Later, some of the attendance come up to talk to Carole and she shows them photos of the wreckage of Mostar and some shrapnel which was taken from a young girls back. Suddenly the war is in the room as they weigh the piece of metal in their hands and they can feel the thump and crunch as it tears flesh and bone. Some shudder at the thought that a doctor would have to dig it out without an anaesthetic or an x-ray though no one who has not been there can really imagine the screams or see the face contorted with excruciating pain as he probes the open wound for the two inch piece of jagged steel.

As usual she exhorts them to pray and once more the message is in matter of fact tones, pleading just a little, the honesty of her message carried clearly in her words.

The local group has got out the support and the night is both successful and enjoyable. Between the two events there will be about £1,200 to go towards much needed medicines. Carole makes a mental note to ring the wholesalers on Monday and order some essentials which the doctors in Mostar have asked for.

They chat with the local group for a while and eventually board their car for home. They both realise they are hungry as they pass the local late-night take-away and Tony offers to go and purchase. At a quarter to three in the morning the choice is limited and he eventually opts for fish, garlic mushrooms and chips and brings two portions.

Back in the warm car, Whitney Houston is entertaining Carole and she and Tony devour their snack appreciatively. The three o'clock news is just starting as Tony eases the car back on Main St., and they start the seventy five mile trek back to Carrigaline.

The first flashes of lightning cross their path on the outskirts of the town and Tony knows it's going to be a long night.

Drumcollogher is past when they see three young lads on the road. They can be no more than fourteen or fifteen and they trudge along through the rain, looming up quickly in the head lights and barely getting their thumbs extended before Tony would pass.

A quick nod of agreement from Carole and he pulls over. In the cities this age group might be a danger but in the heart of rural Cork a mid-teenager is still an innocent child.

They are coming home from a disco and it's not the first time they have had to walk. They too are going to Broadford, which they continually refer to as Broad and as the miles pass they relax a little. They have been suspicious of Carole and Tony and wonder what they're doing fifty miles from Cork in the middle of the night. It never occurs to them that their presence in the middle of nowhere in the small hours of the morning is anything but normal.

One of the boys has got a date for the following week, making him a target for the others' jokes, but they all enjoy themselves.

Tony opts to detour to see them home and they tell him gaily that he should leave them off in Broad and rejoin the main road lower down.

Before they go they admit that this is a regular night out and that they don't always get a lift. Sometimes they would arrive home at seven in the morning, just in time to do the milking.

Shortly after the boys leave, Carole eases the seat back, wraps a rug around herself and with an imagined rather than a spoken prayer she lapses into unconsciousness.

It has been a long and tiring day. At a time when many others were considering a couple of hours of television in front of a roaring fire, she opted for a second days work. Tony being along was a bonus but occasionally she feels a little conscience-stricken at the imposition on his lifestyle. If it weren't Tony, it might have been her father, her other staunch ally in her enterprise.

Eight extra hours, no overtime rates, not even flat rate and provide your own petrol. Sometimes she feels she must be mad, a little guilty at the use of family finances, hoping there will be no adverse affect on the children.

With Carole asleep, Tony puts on a Rod Stewart tape followed by Garth Brooks. He hums along in time to the melodies and compares the beat of the songs to the swish of the wipers.

Lightning flashes occasionally, but it is still a long way off. Steadily the sturdy car eats up the miles but by five-thirty the long day is beginning to take it's toll. Six miles from home Tony considers pulling over for a rest but decides to keep going. The thought of a warm, comfortable bed is inviting and he redoubles his concentration.

It was with considerable relief that he finally reversed in his drive and gently shook Carole awake.

It occurred to him that at six in the morning it would be quite bright if it were summertime, but there was still one last thing to be done before they went to bed.

As Carole made a final cup of tea for them both, Tony checked the video recorder. Yes, it was there, and as Carole arrived with the mugs, the Coronation Street cat was slinking across the fence on the T.V. screen and the Wileys prepared to unwind after a good days work.

14

"People have forgotten the Power of Prayer"

Though Carole Wiley has dedicated virtually all of her spare time, and much of it which was not spare, in the last three years to helping the people of Peru, Croatia and Bosnia/ Hercegovina, she does not believe that this exempts her from the necessity for prayer. Indeed she considers that because she understands the need for prayer, the value of prayer and has experienced prayer at its most satisfying, she has a duty to pray as often as possible and lead and point others in that direction too.

But hers is not a dictatorial approach whether at home or elsewhere and if she is the one to raise the subject it is only to invite people to join with her in saying one Our Father. This may well lead to more, but she will be happy with just that, one Our Father said with genuine respect and fervour and with a conviction that it will be heard in Heaven.

Many of the people who hear her speak are children in schools, and there too, as she tells them of the horrors of war in Bosnia/Hercegovina, she will invite them to join her in one prayer.

With the younger children, this is rarely a problem and their innocent voices intone with her the words of the Lord's prayer. If she expects any resistance from the more worldly wise of her teenage listeners, who have entered their "cool" phase, they are more than willing to co-operate at the end of her talk.

"There are no atheists in foxholes" is an old but true maxim, and after she has described the horrors of everyday life in Bosnia, the suffering of the people, the tortures, the hunger and her reasoning of the satanic influence, they are more than ready to join her in a prayer for peace and the defeat of Satan.

Time and again teachers stand aside in their classrooms and see their students sit enthralled by her words. After a short few minutes even the class wags, rebels and hard men are listening intently and fifteen minutes later lead a genuine applause as she finishes.

Later in the afternoon she leads them in a prayer service and speaks to almost a thousand teenagers crammed into the Parish Church. She again speaks of the hardships of "this satanic war".

"No man could do what is being done out there unless he were being led by Satan" she tells her attentive young listeners, "and I hate mentioning his name at all, which gives him a kind of glory. That is my main reason for coming here today. Not to tell you the horror stories of Bosnia, but to get you to pray. The most important thing you can do is to come together as a young people and pray for the young people who are suffering out there. Some have lost their parents, others have lost brothers or sisters. Some are totally alone, with no one but friends to take them in and share what little they have with them.

I know we have our poor here in Ireland, but there are agencies which can help. No one need be totally alone, no one need starve, no one need go without medicine.

Do we get tired of hearing about Bosnia? Do we switch off our televisions and say, enough? But the people of Bosnia are living it daily, and we must come together as a people and pray for them in their time of need.

Maybe you go to Mass on Sunday because you were sent from home and, you have to go. You stand at the back, or maybe outside. You feel you are fulfilling your duty but you feel you don't have to go in. I know, I was sixteen too, I know what it is like.

When you come to the Church, make a new resolution to open your hearts to where you are coming and with whom you are going to meet. You are coming to your second home, where your heavenly Father is waiting for you to ask for what you need and He will give it to you. We have forgotten to believe this, we have forgotten the power of prayer.

Mass is the most important prayer you can come to, it is the most important prayer of all and when Jesus walks among you, or comes to you at Communion time, ask Him to move his hand to stop this war and restore peace in the World".

She shows the young people the Croatian Rosary beads which she brings around with her. She exhorts them to get a rosary if they do not own one already or just say the prayers and count on their fingers.

"The people of Croatia and Bosnia/Hercegovina are asking that we join them in prayer, that we pray with them for peace, that Jesus will move His hand to stop this war.

You are the ones who can give good example, to your brothers and sisters. It is you they will imitate in dress, in speech and how you dance. Be a good example to them in prayer too. Let them see you come to church, let them hear you say you are going to the church to pray. Start now and there might be even one young soul you will bring to God.

Search for a vocation and if you do not find one, work as a lay person through prayer groups. Come back to prayer and bring the young people with you".

For that moment at least, some must have been convinced, but for how long the message stayed with them Carole will not know. She is content to think that if even one of those young people was inspired to a better prayer life, that if the effect of her homily was to last but one day, the journey and effort would have been worthwhile.

The children have been asked to bring one item of food each for the hungry of Mostar and as they file out they deposit the tin or packet or box in collection bins at the back of the church. One girl drops in her items and carries on towards the door. Suddenly

191

she pauses, feels her pocket, turns around again and deposits what is obviously her own bar of chocolate in the box. From the moment she got the idea it was obvious she was committed to the gift and weeks later in some village of Bosnia/Hercegovina, maybe some little child, whose hair would be blonde if it could be washed, enjoyed a chocolate bar like no Irish child ever could.

There are many simple acts of kindness from many people in Ireland, not least among the young, and without their help the Carole and Áine Appeal could not have been as successful as it has been.

But what is the philosophy of this everyday housewife who has the usual responsibilities of mother and wife, who has accepted the extra burden of aid worker and who hopes to resume as pilgrimage organiser when this dreadful war is over.

What is the code by which she lives, or at least to which she aspires? From where does she get her inspiration? What are the ground rules of her life?

"Rather than just reading The Gospel people have to bring it to life. When Jesus inspired those writings by His life here on earth, He did not want them as just words in a book, to be read and put down. He gave us ideas, ways of living and treating each other so that we can live in harmony together. To live in His peace.

When someone is hungry you feed them, when someone is thirsty you give them a drink, when you see someone naked you dress them. These are the words He gave us and in practical Christian terms today, this is what we must do.

But we must assist all our good deeds with prayer and this is the most important aspect of life today. We do not always pray properly, exchanging quality for quantity, trying to pack as many rosaries as we can into our prayer time.

We bombard heaven, we ask, we beg, we plead, we thank Him for a variety of favours. Someone may be sick or dying, we may need material goods, there are exams to be passed. We are always talking and so often we do not listen.

Silence can sometimes be the best prayer of all. A time when we can sit and listen to God. Sometimes we talk too much, whether in ordinary conversation or in prayer. God gave us two ears and just one mouth, maybe we should listen a lot oftener than we speak.

It is easy to pray in Medjugorje, there is something special about the place, it cannot be described, it needs to be experienced. When people ask me what it is like, all I can tell them is; go there and see and experience for yourself.

I have got the same feeling in some churches here at home. Some churches have a good atmosphere and it is easy to slip into a prayerful mood. My favourite time to pray in church is when it is empty and often I will go in just before it closes. It is unfortunate that because of vandalism and theft many of our churches are closing very early in the evening and often during the day. But when it is quiet and peaceful it is lovely to sit or kneel and listen for what God has to say to me.

In Medjugorje prayers and celebrations can run late into the evening and the church may not close until midnight. Even after that, people would still get together outside under the dome of the church to sing hymns, pray and be together. It is a beautiful atmosphere and you feel very much in the presence of God.

You pray with different people whom you have never met before. A bond builds between you and there is a strong feeling of harmony and togetherness. It is a spiritual closeness, a closeness which allows you to open up to friends and discuss God and spirituality. That too is prayer and something you could not readily do here at home or outside of a small number of locations.

It is easy to have faith in Medjugorje or Lourdes or other places of special devotion. There, we do not have our everyday responsibilities of home, husband and children who have to be catered for every other day of the year. But we must remember too, that doing our everyday duty whatever that might be, is prayer in itself.

193

I think it is the Cistercians who embrace the principle "Laborare est Orare", To work is to pray, and of course our first responsibility is to our duty, whatever that might be. That for me is for fifty one weeks of the year, but the fifty-second is for me, my God and His Mother and it is a time I treasure greatly.

It is a time when I can be alone for some hours of the day at least, and everyone needs that space to be alone with their God to deal with the everyday problems of life. It is essential to have time to think and evaluate the problems and come up with answers and solutions, or at least an acceptance.

You may not hear a voice boom down at you from the clouds, but you will get an answer, that I know. Remember the people of Medjugorje have their work to do, their own problems to solve and now a war to deal with. Despite all of this, they still meet in the church at six o'clock. The men come from the fields or their places of work, the women come from their homes, the children come from their play.

This is their meeting place. Here they join together in prayer and afterwards everyone goes home to their evening meal. This was a practice from long before the Apparitions started, though in those days they would meet at five o'clock.

There is still Rosary, Mass, the healing of the sick and whatever other celebrations there might be. These normally go on until nine o'clock or so and then there is the evening meal. After that there is time for rest, but many choose to climb Apparition Hill, even that late at night and will continue to pray until two o'clock in the morning. It is a beautiful time.

Coming back to Ireland after that kind of lifestyle can be a change. You want to bring the peace, the devotion, the access to prayer, home with you, which you have experienced for the last week, but suddenly there are all those extra responsibilities at home. It is not going to be possible to have the same spiritual life as you enjoyed in Medjugorje and this brings you down to earth quite quickly. So it is necessary to be able to see motherhood as a vocation, to be part of His plan. To put it in modern terms, work of equal value. To see it as any less would be not to acknowledge reality".

What does she pray for when she approaches the altar?

"Wisdom. I will not pray for the things we sometimes feel we should have, though of course if anyone in the family is sick or has troubles, we pray for them. But if you have wisdom you will shed many of the other problems which stem from not living wisely. I pray for my children, that I can rear them properly. These are times when it is difficult to bring prayer into young peoples lives.

For our generation it was different. There was great emphasis on prayer and the rosary in most homes. It was automatic that there was family prayer and it was accepted, if sometimes not very gracefully, by the children. Now there are many distractions. There is little room in the world of 1994 for prayer, and despite being able to save enormous time by having machines, computers and every conceivable labour saving device, there never seems to be a natural time for prayer.

It has to be provided for. Each evening is different and if the moment passes it is lost. Science seems to be pushing out God. Our ten year olds can debate about our evolving from animals, and the foundation of the world and everything seems to point towards the non-necessity for God. Simplicity is gone, there is no childhood, no natural vacancy for God. It has to be created, worked on and always emphasised.

The most important thing to pray for is the gift of forgiveness, the ability to forgive, for if we do not forgive, how can we expect our Father in Heaven to forgive us. With that too we must also have the ability to put others first in every situation. We do not always do that, chasing ahead and doing things our own way, suffering the guilt afterwards".

But surely if she were to wait to please everyone in the collection of aid, many would be dead before even one container would arrive in Bosnia. Sometimes it is necessary to work with purpose, a kind of single-mindedness which does not take account of others. Does she not accept that in feeding the hungry, and clothing the naked of Bosnia, that she is doing it "to these the least of my brethren", and that she is doing it for the Lord.

"Yes of course, I believe that, and when I get tired and need refreshment I take great consolation from those words in the bible. I know He is around me and even when I go to Mostar and am frightened touching down in the war zone I feel a protective blanket around me and know that I am clothed in His love.

I trust in Him to help me get the aid out. Without it many would suffer. Fear comes only from Satan and we must rise above it and place ourselves in God's hands. I know now I was put here for a purpose, was chosen in Medjugorje and have fulfilled that calling by my work for the cold and hungry of Bosnia.

We are given options. We have a choice of what to do with our lives and it is up to each one of us to fulfil our own destiny. I feel I am fulfilling mine. There are many roads to God, some long, some short, some smooth, some rugged. The one we choose is our own decision, and sometimes we stray. But the vast majority come back on the right road again somewhere further along.

Not all rejoin the right path, not least those people who today either knowingly or otherwise are committed to Satan, through a variety of different groups. I know it is not fashionable to talk about Satan these days, and many people have ceased to believe in him, but we only have to see the evil in the world, in Bosnia and elsewhere, even in Ireland, to know that there has to be an evil one behind it all.

There are many satanic groups who make sacrifice in one form or another and who continue to dabble in matters which they may not fully realise are not just wrong but dangerous.

These have to be fought and the only way is through prayer. People have forgotten the power of prayer, that Jesus has told us Himself "Ask and you shall receive". Often their attitude can be summed up as 'it is the will of God'. They might as well not pray at all with an attitude like that. Pray with a purpose, ask for something, for healing, for wisdom or for forgiveness. Your prayer will be granted and then say thank you. It may not be answered at the time or in the fashion you have asked for, but it will be answered and perhaps in a better way than you can ever imagine.

For me the crucifix is the focal point, the very centre of my prayer life. Whether that should be or whether I should concentrate more on the Risen Christ, I sometimes wonder. When I see the crucifix I have a desire to lift His arms and ease the burden, take the strain, give Him a little rest for a few moments. I can visualise myself lifting Him just to get the pain from his hands. I can see the suffering in His face and all I want is to ease it for a moment.

I explained this for the first time two years ago to a priest in Medjugorje and said how I would love to approach the Crucifix and lift His arms to ease the pain in His hands. He replied that through the work I was doing, and the people I was helping that I was already easing His pain. For the first time I really knew the meaning of those words from scripture, 'Inasmuch as you did it to these the least of My Brethren you did it to Me' and it was a great consolation for me.

Suddenly all the work was worthwhile, not just the containers of aid, but previously in the people I had taken to Medjugorje on pilgrimage. In that peaceful place many have found peace if not physical healing, have found reconciliation for the first time in decades, have found the courage to die with dignity.

All who have helped in this effort get these benefits too, not least my family who have contributed in what they have missed. Time I should have spent with them, I spent filling containers. Evenings I might have been with them by the fireside I have been on the road collecting. Special moments have gone by for them without my being around.

But look at the choice. People dying of starvation, cold and lack of the most basic medicines against children who also have a good father, grandparents and many relations and friends, who have a relatively comfortable lifestyle and good prospects for the future.

If we had more help, I could be at home more, and I look forward to the time when we have more hands than we have work for. Perhaps it's something I should pray for more often, but the children do not complain and they understand that the work I am doing is necessary and urgent. They help out at busy times and get a feeling of satisfaction from knowing they have contributed their share.

My favourite prayer is the Our Father, and it is one I say over and over again, slower each time. I have learned that it is better to say one prayer well than a hundred without any thought or concentration or feeling. One prayer from the heart with all the love and energy you can find is better than all the rest.

Music and hymns in church I find very valuable, very stimulating and if the mood is right, if the hymns are right and the choir is on song then there is nothing can compare. It lifts me to the very heavens and I am transported to Calvary, and to the Tomb on Easter Morning. I love to join with the choir in the hymns and for me it is a very positive and tangible aspect of our adoration of our God".

She has had an opportunity to join in some of that music and prayer on an Easter Monday. 1993 has been a violent year in Ireland and there has been an upsurge in interest in a peace movement which has been inspired and led by Susan McHugh.

Carole has been asked to attend a Day of Prayer for Peace to be held on top of a small mountain in the foothills of the Comeraghs. On top of Cruachán is a huge cross which has been erected by the local parish as a reminder of their pilgrims visits to Medjugorje and the peaceful hours they had spent on Mt. Krizevac.

It is called the Cross of Hope and Peace and as a destination for a peace walk with the rosary being recited along the way, it is especially appropriate.

There is a huge turnout and even though there has been torrential rain in the days previously the use of a new service road should ensure the safety of the pilgrims.

Slowly the thousand or so who have given up their Bank Holiday wend their way up the mountain, united in prayer and hymns. The panoramic view is distracting but by the time the final stragglers have reached the top the clouds have closed in and a thick mist has begun to wet the pilgrims.

"Think of the people of Ulog and how they have to live", Carole tells the crowd "and they don't even have a decent roof over their heads. But they live on top of a mountain just like this and have been living in cowsheds for the last eight months.

We have been able to answer their plea for material help, but peace, their great desire, can only come through united prayer.

But with all the suffering these people have had to endure they never lost their faith. Though sometimes they have lost heart and wondered if Heaven had forgotten them, deep down, they have never lost the faith, which like the people of Ireland, has sustained them for centuries.

Here in Ireland when we come to church we sometimes do not even get past the front door. In Bosnia/Hercegovina where the people are suffering terribly they cannot get close enough to the altar, they cannot get close enough to Jesus. They will sit on the steps of the altar to get as close to Him as possible and they will pray the Our Father with hands linked with the people beside them. This is the prayer which Our Father Himself gave us and is our most important prayer.

They enjoy their faith, they live it to the full and they are not afraid to show joy amidst the sorrows they are suffering. At Communion time they flock to meet Him and as they receive Him on their tongues they plead with Him for peace. Without their faith, they would be totally lost".

The rain is now coming down in great sheets and after more hymns and prayers the pilgrims scatter to their cars and their homes.

How nice it would be, she thinks, if the people of Bosnia/Hercegovina were able to run back to their warm homes, return to their families, resume their work. It will be some time before they can do that and for many the opportunity will never come again. She is sad as she reaches the bottom of the mountain. Hillsides always remind her of Mt. Krizevac and Apparition Hill and the good times she has had among good friends.

As she meets Tony and her Co. Waterford friends, she marvels at how many have taken the trouble to come, to pray for peace in Ireland and Bosnia and who renewed their memories of Medjugorje.

She promises herself she will be back and will remember this place the next time she is on Apparition Hill.

15

TRUCKS AND TROLLEYS

"Another container-load of supplies left the Carole Wiley Appeal Warehouse today bound for Mostar in war-torn Bosnia/Hercegovina. The forty foot container which is the thirty fifth to leave the Cork Marina Appeal headquarters was filled with equal quantities of food, medical supplies and clothes and will reach the beleaguered people of besieged Mostar in eight days time. All the aid was donated free and came from several areas of the country".

That news item may or may not have been carried on an Irish radio station early in 1994, but it is similar to the concise report a journalist might file if she were covering the departure of one of the truck loads of humanitarian aid, collected, processed and packed by Carole and her family, friends and supporters all over the country.

It would be impossible to deduce from those words the long hours spent in supermarkets, the chilling, numbing nights spent sorting clothes and food items in the warehouse, the bone wearying trudge between warehouse and truck with hundreds of boxes, sacks and the many items of furniture which go to make up a consignment.

The hearts of the Irish people are large and while their pockets may not always be full, they are still willing to share what is in them. It may be in the form of food, clothes, bedding, cups and saucers or money, but a share will always be set aside for the needy.

It annoys Carole to read criticisms of the people of Ireland, that all they think about are handouts, whether from the State or Europe and that there is still religious intolerance here. She has yet to meet anyone during an appeal who will question the destination of the aid, who will even think about its division between Christian and Muslim with some Serbs being beneficiaries as well. Some may wonder about the Irish needy, but Carole will reassure them that there are individuals, voluntary organisations and State agencies to help them.

"Lets fill a container" might be the eager cry of a group anxious to lend their support to Carole's Campaign and send something to the Bosnian people which will ease their hunger, guard them against cold and raise their spirits just a little if only for a day. There is much more to it than that.

Those who take on such a task had better be strong, for the work is long and arduous, rewarded only by the satisfaction of knowing that they are the present day Samaritans and did not pass those in need.

As the food comes in from a supermarket appeal it must be sorted and packed ready for the pallet. From early on Carole used only forty foot containers which are more economical to send on their long journey through Europe and it is difficult for the uninitiated to imagine the enormous capacity of these monstrous juggernauts. Forty feet represents the length of an average bungalow and it's eight feet height is the standard height of a modern ceiling. At eight feet wide it has the capacity of about forty percent of the volume of a house. It is intimidating to look inside and regardless of how much material is lying in the warehouse there is always a doubt that there will be enough.

It has room for twenty pallets each stacked with boxes to about six feet high and from there to the ceiling is usually packed with sacks of clothes. No space is wasted, no nook or cranny left unfilled.

There is rarely a shortage of clothes and it never ceases to amaze the volunteers the quantity which is handed in to the warehouse and the various collection points around the country.

202

Wardrobes and drawers are cleaned out, out of date clothes discarded and in some cases, some of the best stock selected to give away. In a minority of cases people take the opportunity to dump unwanted clothes, furniture or household items and it no longer surprises Carole the number of people who will "donate" items which should - and subsequently do - go to the dump.

"If you wouldn't wear it yourself then don't ask anyone in Bosnia to wear it either" is Carole's motto. "They may be homeless, they may be poor, but let us at least leave them their dignity".

When kitchen-ware is appealed for, it brings a shower of good cups, saucers, plates, pots and pans. But invariably in their midst will be cracked plates, cups without handles and blackened saucepans.

Some people can be very selfish but thankfully the vast majority of people make a generous contribution, often far more than they can afford in a particular week and on average far more than their European neighbours.

The evidence of the generosity of people which lies in front of the volunteers in the form of food, medicine and blankets is enough to lift their spirits and Carole tells them that they will feel good as they see the container head for the docks and Bosnia.

They set to with a will and the new helpers are schooled by Carole in the art of filling a box. First, she explains, the box should not be too big as more than likely the pallets will be unloaded in Mostar by women. Among them will be Áine, probably Carole herself and other helpers at the hospital and by the time they have carried their fiftieth or sixtieth box into the warehouse, running to be finished and away from possible snipers, they are out of breath and their backs are killing them.

The volunteers understand and pack the boxes with a layer of tinned food covered with baby cereals, packet soups or porridge. Once when she explained this to a group, they murmured that she was stretching the food to make it look bigger but she refrained from wishing that they could feel the hair stand on their necks as they worked within range of snipers and mortars. On many occasions, food queues, humanitarian aid stations and water taps were targeted and Carole has video footage of the aftermath of such an attack. The pictures are not pretty. You don't linger in the open in Mostar.

As the boxes are filled, taped and labelled to show their contents, they are stacked on the appropriate pallets and slowly the piles of food, medical items and clothes grow.

It is tiring work and the more so when the number of workers is small. Over sixty boxes fill a pallet and that multiplied by eighteen makes a huge number of boxes to be filled, stacked, marked and matched if they are not of uniform size. After several hours, weariness sets in. The workers have had their days work already either at home or in the workplace and by eleven o'clock everyone is ready for bed.

Unfortunately that is not possible on this occasion as some of the anticipated food for the consignment was late arriving from the donor town and the container has to be packed to leave the following day. Wearily they continue to work, joking with each other until finally they fall silent, working by rote, almost like automatons with only previous experience keeping them going correctly.

As the pallets are filled they are wrapped in heavy duty cling wrap to keep the boxes together. It demands strong arms and an ability not to get dizzy as the reluctant volunteer runs backwards in circles around the pallet wrapping as she goes, keeping the polythene tight, turning it at intervals to strengthen the binding.

Finally the pallets are pulled on trolleys to the finished area to be taken by forklift the following morning to the waiting container. All these skills had to be discovered, learned and perfected over a number of consignments.

In the midst of all this is Carole who continually juggles the details in her head like a computer going through possible combinations and permutations. Mentally she allocates the pallets to their places in the container. First in, will be two light pallets of clothes followed by two heavy pallets of food. She works out a balanced load, leaving room for the hospital beds and lockers which arrived in the warehouse that day from Waterford. Space has to be allowed too for the fourteen stacking chairs which arrived from the convent and which will be eagerly claimed at destination.

The four full pallets which arrived from the food company have to be kept until last as they will have to be inspected by customs for export refund. The potatoes will be have to be accessible too, to be taken out and given time to breathe in Rotterdam so that they do not sprout and spoil. They were donated by growers and distributors and will be in great demand in Mostar.

The sacks of clothes are sorted and ready and Carole will instruct the loaders in the morning if they are new to such a load, not to throw the bags as they are likely to burst. This would slow down unloading in Rotterdam and Mostar, possibly spoiling the clothes donated with a good heart in Ireland.

Carole occasionally asks people in the donor towns to put in something identifiable which can be photographed in Bosnia as proof of the arrival of the truck. Sometimes some of the garments can look a little incongruous in their new country particularly tee-shirts with Irish logos, slogans or names. She recalls a story Áine told her some time before. Áine had been in Mostar delivering aid when a bout of shelling started and she dived for cover. Across the road, a house was hit and out dashed a man wearing only tee-shirt and shorts. For a moment he was frozen in Áine's gaze as he crossed the road towards her and she had time to read   "Paddy _____, Mullingar Golf Club" emblazoned across his chest.

The incongruity of it suddenly struck Áine and in the midst of the shelling she started laughing. She regretted not having a camera just then, the photo would have scooped any journalistic award though she does not always agree with the local population being photographed by aid workers.

Some groups are less than sensitive to the feelings of the people of Bosnia when they ask them to pose for photos or video footage. One such incident caused outrage amongst the local community when children were asked to run towards a particular aid worker, in full view of the video camera calling the workers name.

"We have our dignity too" the parents said and the food they received must have carried a bitter taste at the evening meal.

Some of the oddest items have made their way to the appeal warehouse, none more so than the four hearses which arrived in quick succession in the Spring of 1994. Oddly enough they provided a humorous moment during Carole's interview on the Gay Byrne Show. As Carole spoke of sending out a hearse, the pronunciation suggested to Gay that she had said horse. "Is Shergar going to Bosnia" asked Gay. "He wouldn't last long" replied Carole, "he'd be quickly eaten".

However the hearses came in useful as ambulances and for ferrying the aid between hospitals and refugee camps. While they were used in death here in Ireland, they were more associated with life in Bosnia. Later she was promised an ambulance which, when it arrived would more than earn its keep on the streets of Mostar.

On one occasion there was a beautiful wall clock in traditional style donated with the stipulation that it should go to a needy person in Bosnia. The donor's wish was granted and it now hangs proudly on a wall in Mostar.

Some went the extra mile with their gift, like the woman who presented a cot fully dressed and ready for a child. Children were even more thoughtful and generously donated their toys. Some gave wind up cars and animals which did not require batteries or mains electricity, both of which are in very short supply in Bosnia.

One young class at school collected all their sweets on Ash Wednesday, put them in a specially decorated box which they all signed and sent with all the love they could muster. Even if the language were strange to the children of Bosnia, the message was nonetheless clear.

Another family decorated a child's lunch-box which they filled with sweets and sent to some less fortunate family in

Mostar or Ulog. Few actually realise the value of this treat for children who not alone have not had sweets for two years, but more often than not have not had enough food either.

Between food appeals which she herself would conduct, Carole would receive aid from other towns and villages directly into the warehouse. Sometimes she would have to go and collect it from the groups herself. Dressed in sweater, jeans and trainers she would jump in and out of the lorry cab in the easy style of a long distance trucker and help load the aid which had been collected on her behalf.

She would take that opportunity to meet some of the people who had campaigned for aid for her and would thank them personally and ask them to continue their efforts on behalf of the people of Bosnia.

Though she has most of the operation streamlined at this stage and has eliminated any waste of time or effort, filling a container is still a major task. Conscious that she spends too much time in the warehouse sorting and packing, when she should be doing what she does best, getting people to work for Bosnia, nevertheless she likes to show solidarity with her workers and stay in touch with the real work of the campaign. She can readily sympathise with her helpers in other towns who have undertaken the task of doing the work for her and she knows their weariness as they pack the last of their goods behind one closed door of their container.

On one such occasion, as the doors were being closed, a ten year old, accompanied his mother, came into the warehouse and handed over his gift to be loaded. He presented two Tonka trucks which must have been his pride and joy and without a murmur and with a ghost of a smile he saw them packed safely in.

Carole and the local group together close and seal the doors, to be opened next in Rotterdam by the drivers who have come up in their lorries to meet the container. A local priest blesses the work, the aid and the driver and vehicle, as they stand ready to go.

As the engine revs up and the emotion takes over in the workers, they suddenly know that it has all been worthwhile, an investment in people, in their sisters and brothers in a foreign land.

As the truck disappears into the distance, one volunteer remarks "Carole was right you know, it does make you feel good" and who would know better than the woman who has sent countless trucks of life giving aid across the seas.

16

THE FUTURE

The future for Bosnia/Hercegovina is something which Carole dreads even to contemplate. Early 1994 saw the beginning of hope that the war might soon be ended. The signs, though small and weak, were encouraging, and if the progress of the first three months were maintained peace might come to that ravaged land by midyear. The U.N. threat of airstrikes had become a little more credible and there were signs that the price of a Greater Serbia might be too high to sustain.

The U.N. appeared for the first time to be keeping Serbia in check on one side and on the other Croatia was pulling its troops back home.

Peace negotiator Lord David Owen appeared not to have any new initiative, and seemed to hold little sway over the Serbs. Whatever proposals he had, had either been rejected or left to die a natural death unlike the thousands of victims of the war who had died in the previous two years.

How long more would humanitarian aid be needed in Bosnia/Hercegovina? How long more could Carole sustain her effort which had taken a huge toll on her in the previous two years. How long more would the people of Ireland be prepared to donate food and money? Would a new international blackspot emerge which would attract the worlds attention and their humanitarian assistance. Surely some nation would feel sufficiently conscience-stricken to raise the plight of Bosnia/Hercegovina in realistic form in some World forum. Could the new European Union to which Slovenia, Croatia and

Bosnia/Hercegovina intended applying for membership, continue to sit on the sidelines and do nothing? Would some member of the United Nations Security Council sponsor some realistic plan for the former Yugoslavia.

All those wishes had been wished for in the last two years, and nothing had happened. All Carole knew was that as long as she could continue to be effective, she would continue her work. She just hoped her family would continue to be patient, to understand the desire in her and the need of the people. Her own children were growing up, and she was pleased with their progress. She knew from things she had heard that they were proud of her and this was a necessary affirmation of her work. Sarah continued to tell her so, and Mark had made her the subject of his essay on "The Kindest Person I Know" for which he had been commended in school and which he had been invited to read to the entire school at assembly.

Audrey, perhaps the most generous and sensitive of the family understood the need to look after the suffering children whose parents had been killed in the war, just as when she had fed as a child, Carole's freshly baked biscuits to her young friends because they did not have any that day.

Kristian, like any six year old, could not even begin to understand about a war a thousand miles away, but he could identify with children with no parents, no home, no toys, no sweets and would play a man's part in the warehouse. Carole hoped he would look back on his childhood with understanding and realise that because of the Wileys, other people had been given a chance in life.

The ever patient Tony was content to accommodate the work which was important to Carole. He acted as part-time chauffeur, accountant, receptionist and advisor, and more important, full time father to the family. Carole would be confident of him, rely on him, lean on him and often privately admit to Jan that he was a candidate for sainthood.

She knew she could rely on her husband, her family and her parents, and she loved them dearly for it.

Her friendship with Áine had endured a war and a distance of a thousand miles and Carole looked forward to a time when peace would descend once again on Bosnia/Hercegovina and allow Áine and Toni to get on with their lives. In war or peace, she would have her friendship with Áine and they had been through a lot together in Ireland and Bosnia.

If the war continued, Carole promised she would sustain her effort as long as possible. If prayers for peace were successful, she would resume the pilgrimages. She prayed regularly that Áine and Toni would have a long and happy life together.

She looked forward to getting back to normality, to spending more time with her own family, her sisters and brothers, nieces and nephews who are now growing up and whom she does not see as often as she would like, particularly her eldest godchild Victoria now in College.

With this book out of her system, she knows that there are other subjects with which she would like to deal. The war had drawn her into public life, had thrown a spotlight on her and made her a kind of public property. She realises that there are needy in Ireland too, though not to the same extent as in Bosnia today. In time she would like to be able to do something for those people as well. Her days and nights on the road gathering aid, speaking to groups in draughty halls, and in schools which needed repairs, showed her the deficiencies in our society and she has her own ideas on how these wrongs can be put right.

As she reflected on the pattern of the previous seven years, her pregnancy, her visit to Medjugorje, Vicka's kiss, her vision, the war and the appeal, she marvelled that she could never have anticipated how her life could have changed so drastically from anything she could have envisaged. and she wondered what the next seven years would bring.

Acknowledgements.

The author wishes to thank the following for their invaluable assistance :

Cork City Library,
Waterford County Library,
County Waterford V.E.C.
Carrigdhoun Weekly,
Copy Type, Dungarvan,
Cork Examiner Publications,
Data Systems Ltd. Dungarvan,
Aine de Burca,
Gay Byrne Show, R.T.E.,
Mr. Maurice Gubbins, Cork Examiner Publications,
The Lord Mayor of Cork, Cllr. John Murray.
Rev. Sean O'Driscoll,
Mr. Eamonn Timmins, Cork Examiner Publications,
Sanjin Velic,

to

Mary and Tony, for their encouragement and advice,
Tom Keith (Jnr.), for his computer skills,
The Wiley Family, for their warm friendship and hospitality,
and
my wife Carmel, for her unfailing patience and support.

C.W.B.A.

Carole Wiley Bosnia Aid

Donations to:

C.W.B.A. Account Bank of Ireland, Carrigaline

A/C 40497138